The

LIFE & TIMES of GEORGETOWN SEA CAPTAIN
ABRAM JONES SLOCUM
1861–1914

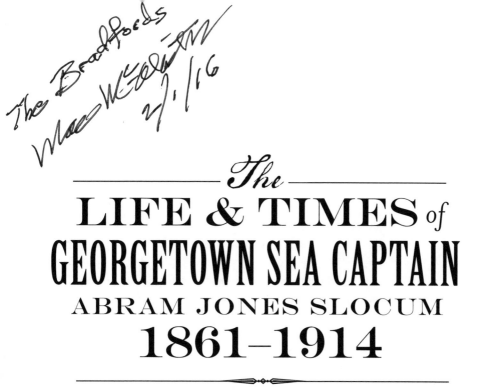

The

LIFE & TIMES of
GEORGETOWN SEA CAPTAIN
ABRAM JONES SLOCUM
1861–1914

ROBERT McALISTER

Charleston   London

THE
History
PRESS

Published by The History Press
Charleston, SC 29403
www.historypress.net

Cover image: Painting of the *Henrietta*, the largest sailing ship built in South Carolina. The unidentified artist has the initials "B.T.N." and was possibly a member of the family of Captain J.C. Nickels, managing owner and first commanding officer of the *Henrietta* in 1875. *Courtesy of Penobscot Marine Museum.*

First published 2012

Manufactured in the United States

ISBN 978.1.60949.787.3

Library of Congress CIP data applied for.

They that go down to the sea in ships, that do business in great waters; these see the works of the Lord and his wonders in the deep.
—*Psalms, 107*

Contents

PREFACE AND ACKNOWLEDGEMENTS

This is a story of the life and times of Captain Abram Jones Slocum. He was part of that last generation of iron men who served aboard and commanded America's commercial wooden sailing ships. The development of steam-powered iron vessels in the mid-1800s brought to an end a history of thousands of years of oceangoing wooden ships powered only by sail. The last gasp of wooden sailing ships occurred in the late 1800s and early 1900s, when three- and four-masted schooners transported lumber and other bulk cargoes from southern ports like Georgetown, South Carolina, around Cape Hatteras at all times of the year to booming cities of the Northeast. Slocum was a Yankee ship captain, an adventurer doing a dangerous business, who loved and was loved by Georgetown, South Carolina.

Without the help of the Georgetown County Digital Library, the Maine Maritime Museum, the New Bedford Whaling Museum and the Penobscot Marine Museum, this book would not have been possible. I would also like to thank Kim Kaminski, Glennie Tarbox and Susan Sanders of the South Carolina Maritime Museum for their help. Also, thanks to Adam Ferrell and the staff of The History Press. I appreciate the help and patience of my wife, Mary Prevost Shower McAlister, and our sons, Jamie, Robert and Charlie McAlister.

Chapter 1

BORN AND RAISED AT SEA

(1861–1881)

Abram Slocum and his twin sister, Myra, were twelve days old when they and their mother, Lydia Slocum, were able to leave the house where she had given birth to them. The house was near the harbor of Horta, on the island of Faial, in the Azores Islands of the Atlantic Ocean. They rode in a wagon to a wharf, where a whaleboat from their father's ship was waiting. Four men of the crew of the *Swallow* rowed Mrs. Slocum and her two babies out to the anchored ship. They were handed up a ladder to the deck, taken to the aft cabin and bundled into a crib that had been built for them by the ship's carpenter. Captain Frederick Slocum looked down at the twins, hugged his wife and smiled. He was a rough giant of a man, over six feet tall and forty years old. His face was deeply weathered and his eyes bright blue. He and Lydia, who was twenty-four, had been married less than a year. She had been a schoolteacher in New Bedford when he met her, soon after his first wife died. He was pleased that she had agreed to accompany him on this voyage. She was a slender, pretty woman with raven hair that she kept piled on top of her head. She had a hard time on board at first, with seasickness and morning sickness. She had suffered another hard time ashore delivering the twins. Frederick wanted his wife and her babies to be as comfortable as he could make them for the rest of the voyage. It was September 28, 1861, when they were all settled aboard the *Swallow*. The anchors were raised and she was underway, heading southeast toward the Canary Islands and along the west coast of Africa.

The whaling bark *Swallow*, built in 1856, drying sails in New Bedford. *Courtesy of New Bedford Whaling Museum.*

Frederick Slocum had grown up along the waterfront of New Bedford, Massachusetts, and had been going to sea in whaling ships since he was a boy. There were times when he had seen as many as forty whaling ships tied up at the wharfs of New Bedford or anchored in the harbor, unloading oil or preparing for the next voyage. He had served on board ships, rising from ordinary seaman to mate and then to captain of the bark *Saratoga*. Now, he was captain of the *Swallow*. He had served on ships where voyages had lasted two or three years. He had rounded Cape Horn and the Cape of Good Hope and had cruised in the Indian Ocean, the Pacific and the China Sea. He had taken hundreds of whales and seen many more get away. He had lost good men when whales stove in their boats. He had been through storms all over the world and had seen men lost overboard. He knew no other life, and he loved the adventure and beauty of the sea. Now he, his family and a crew of thirty men were on their way toward the Cape of Good Hope. They intended to round the southern tip of Africa and hunt for whales in the South China Sea.

Frederick Slocum was a careful man. He knew whaling was a dangerous business, and he took no more chances than necessary, especially now that his wife and babies were on board. Lydia was a brave woman but had never been on such a voyage. He wanted to sail the *Swallow* through the North Atlantic as quickly as possible. Ever since Lincoln's election and the secession of Southern states, armed privateers from Virginia and the Carolinas were boarding Yankee whalers and forcing them into Southern ports to be converted into Rebel warships. Slocum wanted to sail far away from the effects of the Civil War. He had no sympathies for either side and considered it foolhardy that the war had been started. He knew that slavery was wrong and that Africans should never have been brought to America in the first place, but he thought the South should have been left alone to deal with its own problem. He had nothing against blacks. He had signed black hands on board his ships, and most of them had made good sailors. His present crew were all good Yankees, mostly New Bedford boys and men, and they were glad to be on this voyage and not conscripted into Lincoln's army. He had signed on five more hands in the Azores, where he had stopped many times. Azores men were always good sailors.

The *Swallow* made good progress, rounded the Cape of Good Hope in November and headed toward the southwest coast of Australia. They had encountered no storms but had seen only a few whales and none close enough to lower the boats. Whales, especially sperm whales, were becoming scarce in all oceans. There were too many ships chasing too few whales. In the 1850s, petroleum, which could take the place of whale oil, had been discovered. With the cost of taking whales going up and the cost of petroleum coming down, demand for whale oil had dropped dramatically. Old whaling ships had been left to rot or been scrapped. Slocum felt he had a good ship, only five years old. The *Swallow* was bark-rigged, 120 feet long, with a 28-foot beam and 17-foot draft. Her gross tonnage was 327. She would hold three thousand barrels of whale oil. On this trip, Slocum hoped to return to New Bedford with oil and whalebone, which had many uses, particularly the baleen for ladies' corsets.

In the back of Slocum's mind was the idea that, if the *Swallow* could cruise in safe waters near the Equator, and if he could catch and trade enough whale oil and bone to satisfy the crew, he would stay between the Molucca Islands and the China Sea until this war was over. Then, he would return to New Bedford. In February 1862, the *Swallow* arrived in the Malay Straits. For the remainder of 1862 and all of 1863 and 1864, the *Swallow* cruised and hunted whales in the Banda Sea and the Celebes Sea. During that time, they saw only a few other American whaling ships.

On occasions, there was the call from the rigging of, "Thar' she blows." At those times, the boats were lowered and the chase was on. If a whale was struck, the men in the whaleboat were often dragged by the whale for miles over the rough sea until the creature tired and was killed by the lance and towed back to the *Swallow*. Sometimes, the whale dove and broke the harpoon or shook it loose and escaped. With a dead whale alongside, the men cut sections of blubber and lifted them to the deck to be rendered in try pots. The oil was stored in thirty-gallon barrels below deck. Usable whalebone was cut and stored.

Lydia's babies thrived onboard the ship. Frederick Slocum was proud to have a son, and he spoiled him as much as he could. Lydia Slocum was a good sailor and grew to love life aboard ship. She had no ship's duties. Sewing, walking on the quarterdeck, writing letters and reading one of the many books she had brought were her regular pastimes. She cared for her babies and began to teach them, much as she would have done ashore. She respected her husband and could see that he was a good leader for his crew. The crew doted over the babies, protected them and made toys and gifts of scrimshaw for them. The black cook fed them well, and as they grew, he made sure they had the best food he could offer. At various times, Captain Slocum ordered the ship to anchor close to an island village to trade with the natives and take on water. Sometimes, he was rowed ashore with Mrs. Slocum to trade for fresh vegetables and fruits. During this voyage, life in the tropics was easy for them.

On one occasion, in 1864, another New Bedford whaling ship, the *Gazelle*, was close enough to anchor and to row Captain and Mrs. Slocum over for a gam. The *Gazelle* had left New Bedford only a few months before, and the Slocums were eager to hear news from the outside world. They found out from Captain Daniel that in 1862, the Union navy had purchased thirty old whaling ships—many of them from New Bedford— filled them with granite stones, sailed them south to Charleston, South Carolina, and purposely sank them in the ship channel to blockade the port. It sounded like a ridiculous idea to Slocum, but he guessed that the owners of the old ships had received enough money from the Union government to make it worth their while. He recognized the names of some of the ships that had been sunk. Daniel said that the ships had been named the Stone Fleet.

Slocum and Captain Daniel traded yarns. Slocum told of his one connection with South Carolina. He had been mate on the whaling ship *South Carolina* in 1849, when she was commanded by Captain Edward Cory. Those were the glory days of whaling. The old *South Carolina* had been built in 1815 in Charleston from live oak and heart pine and was still a stout ship thirty-three years later. She was 306 tons, 91 feet by 28 feet by 14 feet depth. She had sailed out of New Bedford after 1831. They were away from New Bedford for two and a half years and experienced a voyage of greasy luck. They had cruised the southern Indian Ocean and taken sperm whales, humpbacks, right whales and finbacks. Slocum had kept the log, and almost on every page he had made drawings of the tails of whales they had chased and lost and full profiles of the whales they had taken alongside, cut and boiled to store below. They had encountered some bad storms in the high latitudes and had made repairs to damaged yards and torn sails at sea. They had returned to New Bedford in 1851 with a record load of oil, some of it spermaceti, the prized oil from the head of the sperm whale. Later, after a forty-year career, the *South Carolina* finally weakened and was scrapped in 1854. Slocum credited Carolina live oak for the long life of the *South Carolina*.

Captain Daniel said that, because of Confederate raiders, the price of whale oil had risen since the beginning of the war. He thought that they should do well, if they could return safely to New Bedford with their ships full of oil and bone. Mrs. Jane Daniel was glad to see another woman, but she seemed sad. She had lost her only baby a year earlier. She was cheered by a visit to the *Swallow* to see Lydia's young twins. After Lydia and Mrs. Daniel traded books from their libraries, the two ships parted and went their separate ways.

In August 1864, after Slocum had careened the *Swallow* and had her painted well, they set sail, steering west across the Indian Ocean to the French island of Mauritius. In October, they rounded the Cape of Good Hope, sailed north along the west coast of Africa and anchored in Fishing Bay, Angola, awaiting the end of the war. In March 1865, they sailed from Angola to New Bedford, arriving there on April 24, 1865, with over 1,500 barrels of sperm oil and a ton of bone. The Civil War

An 1849 entry in the ship's log of the whaling bark *South Carolina*. *Courtesy of New Bedford Whaling Museum.*

was over that same month. Abram Jones Slocum had spent his first three and a half years at sea.

Frederick Slocum continued to command whaling vessels for five more years, but Lydia stayed behind in New Bedford to care for her children. Frederick found that there was even less demand for whale oil and more scarcity of whales. Steamships had begun whaling in remote parts of the world, and the capital of whaling had shifted to San Francisco, California, from where ships hunted whales in the Arctic Ocean. Slocum retired from whaling in 1871.

He and his wife were self-sufficient individuals who didn't care to be around a lot of people. They decided to build a house off the coast of Massachusetts on the island of Cuttyhunk, which Frederick Slocum's family had owned since the 1600s. Cuttyhunk was a small island with only a few inhabitants, located twelve miles south of New Bedford. It was the westernmost of the Elizabeth Islands, a chain that stretched west from Cape Cod to Buzzards Bay. In 1864, the island had been sold to the Cuttyhunk Fishing Club, a group of New York millionaires who intended to use the island for their pleasure. Frederick had retained one section of the small island. Each time Frederick Slocum had sailed his whaling ship toward her home port of New Bedford, the first islands he passed were Nantucket, Martha's Vineyard and Cuttyhunk. He built his new house on the shore of a protected cove, which had a narrow entrance into Buzzards Bay. From the porch of his house, he could watch the ships leaving and returning to New Bedford. He kept a small steam launch in front of his house, which he used to provide transportation from New Bedford to Cuttyhunk for the New York fishermen and to bring back supplies for his family. He had another smaller sailing and rowing boat for him and Abram to sail. Two other sons, Frederick and Edward, were born to Lydia while they lived on Cuttyhunk.

Captain Slocum knew that there was no future for his sons in whaling, but he told them his sea stories and taught them the ways of boats and the sea. Lydia, however, was determined that her children would have a formal education. She started the first school on the island, located in the tiny village of Gosnold, and taught her children from books that she ordered and were brought to her from New Bedford by Frederick. Lydia was able to develop Abram's interest in reading only by giving him books about the sea, such as *Two Years Before the Mast* and *Robinson Crusoe*. Abram was a bright enough student, but he spent most of his time sailing in the bay and accompanying his father to New Bedford in the steam launch.

He helped his father fish for cod, tend lobster traps, gather quahogs and plant a garden next to their house. When Abram was fourteen, he would row out into the bay alone to fish and was able to supply the family with all the seafood they needed. Sometimes Abram was paid by one of the wealthy New York fishermen—by visiting President Grover Cleveland on one occasion—to chum the water while they fished for bass. As he grew older, Abram became restless and eager to be aboard one of the ships that passed their house on their way to sea.

By the mid-1880s, wooden square-rigged ships had almost become relics of the past. More and more steamships were being used to transport cargo. Most of the steamships were built with iron hulls. Some had auxiliary sails, but even those were disappearing. Almost the only wooden sailing ships that passed in and out of New Bedford were two-masted fishing schooners and three- and four-masted coasting schooners. All of their masts were fore-and-aft rigs with topmasts rising above their lower mainmasts. The coasting schooners were not built for sailing all over the world like whaling ships. They had shallower drafts and were being used to transport bulk cargo, like lumber, ice, salt and coal, up and down the East Coast of the United States and to and from the Caribbean. They required much smaller crews than whaling ships, which made them competitive with steamships. An eight-man crew could sail a 180-foot, four-masted schooner from New England to any southern port and back. The heavy mainsails and anchors were raised with the help of a steam-powered hoisting engine, called a donkey engine, which transmitted power to winches and the windlass, rather than requiring manpower from a big crew. There was no need for many men to climb the rigging and furl sails from yardarms; there were no yardarms. Whenever Abram accompanied his father to New Bedford, he tried to find excuses to go aboard the schooners.

Many of the coastal schooners were being built in the shipyards of Maine, and in 1879, Frederick Slocum, along with several other men from New Bedford, invested in shares of a new three-masted schooner that was being built by the Goss and Sawyer Shipyard in Bath, Maine. Frederick Slocum owned a ½₂ interest in the vessel, which was named the *Warren B. Potter*. The schooner was 350 tons, 126.6 feet long, 32.4 wide and drew 8.6 feet. The distinguishing feature of the schooner was a beautifully carved wooden figurehead in the likeness of Mr. Warren B. Potter, founder of a successful drug and chemical company who, along with his son, owned substantial interest in the ship. The schooner's shallow draft made her ideal for entering ports and rivers in the southeastern United States. She was built to transport lumber, naval stores and other cargo from southern ports to cities in the Northeast. She was registered in New Bedford and was commanded by Captain Benson of New Bedford.

Chapter 2

ABRAM SLOCUM SAILS TO GEORGETOWN, SOUTH CAROLINA

(1882–1885)

Abram Slocum completed his schooling in 1879. Although he had been a reluctant student, Lydia expected him to go to college. Abram was too restless, though, and vowed he would go to sea. During the years 1880 and 1881, Abram crewed on New Bedford fishing schooners, pulling nets on Georges Bank. In 1882, despite Lydia's protests, Frederick Slocum helped his son sign on the *Warren B. Potter* as an able-bodied seaman, with a promise to Frederick by Captain Benson, who was an old friend from whaling days, that Abram would move up to mate when he was qualified. Lydia was against her son leaving home to go to sea, but there was nothing she could do. She would have to concentrate on the education of her other children, especially Frederick Jr., who was showing signs of being a bright and willing student.

Lydia helped Abram pack a sea bag. She insisted he take a Bible and other books she hoped he would read at sea. She had watched him grow into a strong young man, much like his father. He was a little under six feet tall, with muscular arms, a full head of black hair, a full beard and a bright smile. Abram said goodbye to his mother, brothers and sister and stepped aboard his father's steam launch. He promised to come home as soon as he could. Lydia watched with tears in her eyes as the launch passed through the narrow inlet and headed for New Bedford. Abram and his father tied up to a wharf and walked to the train station. The *Potter* was sailing from Bridgeport, Connecticut. Abram said goodbye to his father and stepped aboard the train.

The schooner *Warren B. Potter* under sail. *Courtesy of Maine Maritime Museum.*

It took most of that day to arrive in Bridgeport. He hoisted his sea bag and walked toward a wharf where the *Potter* was supposed to be. Several majestic three-masted schooners were tied up, and there was no mistaking the distinctive carving of Mr. Warren Potter on the bow of the *Warren B. Potter*. Abram walked up the gangway and met Captain Benson and the rest of the crew. He stowed his sea bag in the forward cabin, which he would share with three other seamen. There was little room to store his gear. At suppertime, the cook served a hot meal through the pie hole, which separated the galley from their fo'c'sle quarters. The four seamen sat on benches at a table and began to get to know one another.

The next morning, a harbor pilot came aboard. A hawser was passed to a steam-powered tugboat, and the *Potter* was towed toward the ocean. It was December 1882, a time of year when northeasterly gales might be expected. The *Potter* carried only a partial cargo of bagged coal in the hold and nothing on deck, so she was riding high. The crew was lucky with the wind and had an easier than average passage, making seven knots before a steady northeast breeze. Abram quickly learned his sailing duties. He helped stow the docking lines, set a topsail, ran out the jibs and hoisted a staysail. By the end of the passage, he had performed all the duties that define an ordinary seaman's life: shoveled coal for the engineer, scoured pots for the cook, stood long night watches at the wheel, cleaned cabins, painted, climbed aloft to shift heavy ropes and chains and run forward when the mate ordered him to do a job. Captain Benson seemed pleased by his skill and enthusiasm.

There was one seaman in the fo'c'sle who couldn't do his duty. He was a pale, scrawny man in his forties who had signed on in Bridgeport, claiming to be an experienced seaman. When the mate ordered him aloft, he hesitated and climbed the ratlines very slowly. He was too weak to lift the topsail sheet. He lost his grip and grabbed a shroud, ripping his hand on a loose strand of cable. Abram had to help him down. Captain Benson brought out the medicine chest and sewed the man's hand as he screamed with pain. Abram guessed he had never been to sea and was one of those misfits who ended up on ships because they couldn't find anything they could do ashore.

On the third day, they passed well east of the Cape Hatteras Lightship and turned toward their destination: Georgetown, South Carolina. Toward the end of the sixth day, they spotted Georgetown Lighthouse, a white conical eighty-foot tower built in 1810. It marked the entrance to Winyah Bay, which led to the port of Georgetown, eleven miles up the bay. Captain Benson ordered the port anchor dropped to await a harbor pilot and a tug. At 4:30 p.m., the pilot boat came alongside, and the pilot climbed aboard. He asked Captain Benson whether he really wanted a tug because there was a steady breeze from the northeast. Captain Benson agreed that the *Potter* could sail up the bay toward Georgetown unassisted. They raised the anchor, and the *Potter* moved slowly up the shallow bay under two jibs and the spanker. As they progressed, the wind slackened, blocked by the trees and sand dunes of North Island. After six miles, there was no wind and the tide was running out, so the *Potter* anchored off Fraser Point, where the bay took a turn. Captain Benson and the pilot decided that the *Potter* would stay there for the night and a tug would come down from Georgetown the next morning.

This was Abram's first trip to the South. He noted that the land was flat, with many marshes and trees, mostly pines he thought, along both shores. Darkness came quickly. The anchor lantern was lit. The crew ate supper, swapped yarns for an hour and turned in for the night. The next morning, Abram awoke before 6:00 a.m., pulled on his trousers and jacket and

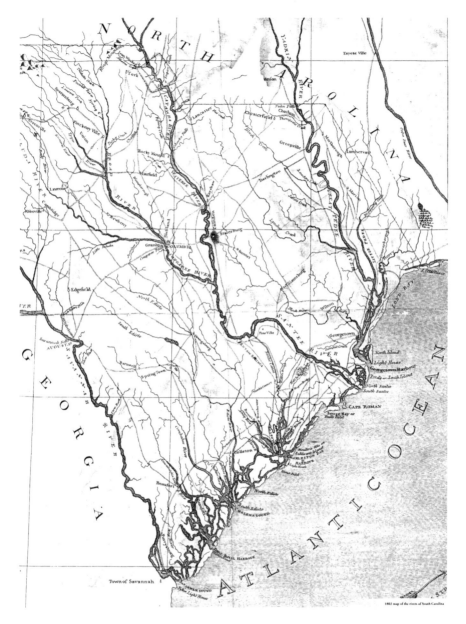

An 1802 map of the South Carolina coast between Charleston and Georgetown. *Courtesy of Georgetown County Digital Library.*

Georgetown Lighthouse, North Island, South Carolina, built in 1810. *Courtesy of Georgetown County Digital Library.*

stepped onto the foredeck. The morning was chilly but nothing like New Bedford in winter. He looked across the bay at a beautiful sky. Wide shafts of pink merged below the horizon well beyond the distant lighthouse. As time passed, he watched the silhouette of a tree line across the bay become more distinct and lighten. Two ospreys called to each other as they glided across the sky. Behind him, he heard an owl and then a killdeer and a dove. The eastern sky lightened to a pale orange, and the pink streaks faded away. Down on the horizon, a darker orange showed where the sun would rise, but not yet for a while. He began to distinguish colors in the marsh grass behind him, dark grays turning to light browns. He heard a rooster and a hunter's distant gunshot. Finally, the sun broke the horizon and the sky was a pale blue. Abram stretched his arms wide and smiled. He was happy on this ship.

The tug and the pilot arrived, the anchor was raised and the *Potter* was towed another three miles to the mouth of the Sampit River and up the river to the town. The tug pushed the *Potter*'s starboard side against a rough wharf, which was barely long enough to throw docking lines to black stevedores on shore. The *Potter* was tied up, bow and stern, with spring lines holding her close to the wharf. There was almost no wind, so Captain Benson ordered some sails raised to dry before giving them a harbor furl. Abram finished his boat chores and was given permission by Captain Benson to go ashore with the starboard watch.

Georgetown didn't look very impressive to Abram. The town stretched out along the river for four or five blocks and ended where the river made a turn to the left. The buildings along the waterfront were mostly two stories high, a few of brick but mostly wood. There was a brick tower with a copper roof that rose above the other buildings. The mate, the engineer, Abram and another seaman climbed onto the wharf and walked through an alley to the main street of the town. The dirt street was fairly wide, with buildings and houses on both sides. There was a live oak tree at the edge of one street, bigger than any oak tree that Abram had ever seen. Gray moss hung from its limbs, which stretched far out in all directions. It was a Saturday, and there were many horses-and-buggies and wagons on the street. Abram had never seen so many black people. They were poorly dressed and walked together, staying out of the way of the white people. The Civil War had been over for less than twenty years. Abram had been told that most southern white people disliked Yankees. Captain Benson had said not to expect friendly greetings, just do your business and move on. He had told the ship's black cook to remain on board because black people from ships weren't allowed on shore.

A view along Georgetown's Front Street from the 1842 clock tower. *Courtesy of Georgetown County Digital Library, Tarbox Collection.*

Abram had a little money that his father had given him, and he wanted to buy a newspaper and some candy. He saw a grocery store and went in. All the people in the store were white and paid no attention to him. He found the candy he wanted and set it on the counter in front of the cashier. He smiled at her and said, "I'm on the ship that just came in. I've never been here before, and it seems like a beautiful town. I was wondering if you could tell me where I can buy a newspaper so I can find out what's going on in the world."

She waited for him to put the money down, took it to the cash register, counted the change, brought it back, put it on the counter, turned her back and walked away. Abram looked around to see if anybody else would respond. Two old ladies walked out of the store. The only other person was a man who turned to him and drawled, "Our newspaper comes out on Tuesday, and it ain't Tuesday." He walked out. Abram had never heard such an accent. He could barely understand what he had said.

"Please, good lady," he said to the saleslady, "I'm only trying to be friendly." Slowly, she turned around. She was a pretty woman, middle-aged, plainly but neatly dressed. She spoke in the same drawl but more softly.

"Maybe you're too young to remember what you Yankees did. Before the war, my family owned a rice plantation on the river and we lived well. You

Yankees came down here and ruined it all. You freed the blacks, and if you stay here long enough, you'll see what you've done. Just leave us alone." She turned her back on him again.

Abram walked out of the store and back to the ship, stunned. He sat on his bunk and thought about what the lady had said. He really knew nothing about the Civil War or southern people. He had never thought about those things. Now, he was going to have to spend part of his life in this unfriendly place. *There must be some southerners who aren't so bitter*, he thought. In time, he would find them. Meanwhile, he would mind his own business and work for the ship.

Black stevedores arrived the next day to unload the bags of coal from the hold. They plodded back and forth in response to commands by a white foreman. When the hold was empty, the *Potter* was warped down the dock to a lumber sawmill. Stacks of heavy timbers were loaded from lighters into the *Potter*'s hold through temporary hatches in the hull, on either side of the bow of the ship and through deck hatches. When the hold was full, the hatches were replaced and sealed against the weather. More lumber was stacked on the main deck until it was level with the top of the rail. The ship was down on her marks, with only about four feet of freeboard. When the deck loading was complete, chains were stretched across the deck lumber and anchored to keep the cargo from shifting in a heavy seaway. The loading of lumber took three days.

Captain Benson had discharged the seaman who wasn't fit and replaced him with a Georgetown sailor. The *Warren B. Potter* was towed to the ocean and got underway, heading for New York City with 300,000 feet of lumber. Abram hoped they would have a fast passage so that he could take a little time off and go home to Cuttyhunk for Christmas. It was not to be. A north wind picked up, and the *Potter* tacked far out to sea, tossed and rolled by steep waves in the very rough Gulf Stream. The captain ordered the lower sails reefed. It was not an easy task to reef the big sails of a schooner, especially at night. The whole crew was called out to do it. The donkey engine's cable was connected to the foresail halyard winch, lowering the foresail and its gaff and boom to the deck. Two men gathered the loose sail below the reef point and tied the reefed sail along the boom. Then the donkey engine engaged the halyard winch and raised the reefed foresail gaff and boom, and the boom was sheeted in to catch the wind. The same process was repeated for the mainsail and spanker. It took almost thirty minutes to reef all the lower sails. When the sails were reefed, the helmsman put the wheel over and tacked the ship.

A steam tug tows the *Warren B. Potter* into port. *Courtesy of Maine Maritime Museum.*

Their progress was slow, and it was after January 1 before they rounded into Sandy Hook and dropped anchor. As snow fell, a steam tug appeared alongside, and the *Potter* was towed toward New York Harbor. It was Abram's first look at the skyscrapers and river traffic of New York City. Despite mid-winter snow and cold, the harbor was alive with boat traffic of all kinds. Steam tugs towed barges, sailing vessels and lighters up and down the harbor. Ferry steamers crisscrossed the harbor. Huge steamships headed out to sea. Abram saw more sailing ships and steamers than he had ever seen in his life. The *Potter* passed Governors Island, under the new Brooklyn Bridge and up the East River to a lumber terminal in Brooklyn. There would be no rest because, as soon as they were unloaded, the *Potter* sailed for Boston to pick up a cargo of ice to be delivered to Norfolk. When the *Potter* tied up in Boston, great chunks of ice were lowered into the hold, and the top layers were covered with straw. When the ice was unloaded in Norfolk, about one-fourth of it had melted. In Norfolk, bagged coal was loaded into the hold of the *Potter* to be delivered to Savannah before sailing back to Georgetown to load more lumber for New York.

Savannah was a better experience for Abram than Georgetown had been. The loading port was far upriver from the ocean entrance. As they were towed up the Savannah River, Abram could see that the city was large and modern. The *Potter* was tied up to a wharf at the bottom of a hill. A cobblestone street and a railroad track ran alongside the wharf. On the far side of the street were blocks of four-story brick warehouses, whose third floors backed up to another street at the top of the hill. A steamboat full of cotton bales was unloading. A big steamship was tied up aft of the *Potter* loading cotton. Ragnar, the Norwegian mate on the *Potter*, offered to show Abram the nightlife of Savannah. Abram wasn't against drinking; he had visited bars along the waterfront of New Bedford to drink ale and listen to the sea stories of whaling crews. Ragnar led them to a bar, almost across from the *Potter*, built into the front of a cotton warehouse. The place was crowded with sailors and locals talking loud and laughing at one another's jokes. Ragnar introduced Abram to a busy bartender, who drew pints and slid overflowing mugs down the polished mahogany bar top in their direction. They stood at the bar and watched reflections of other patrons in the long mirror behind the bar. Barmaids grabbed the handles of two or three full mugs and delivered them to men and a few girls and women who were seated at tables lined up along the rough brick walls of the warehouse building.

At a table in a corner was a beautiful girl facing the mirror behind the bar. Abram watched her, smiling and speaking to the man next to her. She was wearing a long red silk dress and a pretty hat with flowers. Her face was very white, and dark hair pushed out from under her hat. Other men walked by her table and greeted her. *She must be the queen of the bar*, he thought. Abram wished he could meet such a girl and be liked by her. There was no chance of that, he thought. He and Ragnar finished their beers and worked their way through the crowd toward the door. Abram passed close to the girl in the red dress and smiled at her. She met his eye, smiled slightly and turned her head toward another man. Abram felt his day was complete. He and Ragnar visited a few more bars, but Abram's thoughts stayed with the girl in the red dress. About midnight, they returned to the ship. The next morning, their cargo was unloaded, and the *Potter* was towed back down the Savannah River to the sea.

During each passage, Abram gained more experience. He handled the lines, went aloft to shift the topsails, steered the ship and did all the chores and maintenance that was required of an able-bodied seaman. All the training and advice that his father had given helped him to become the most valuable crewman on the ship. He could take a noon sunshot with the sextant as well as or better than the mate. Captain Benson knew that Abram would one day be a captain like his father.

No two passages were the same. During some, they encountered high winds and waves and worked to weather under reefed sails or hove to in a gale. During one passage, a man was lost overboard at night. He fell from the rigging, bounced off the port rail and fell into the sea. He must have been unconscious before he hit the water because he made no sound. The captain ordered the sheets loosed to stop the ship. The yawl boat was put over and rowed around the ship, but they didn't find the man in the darkness. There was nothing to be done but continue the voyage. It was the lost man's first passage on the *Potter*, and none of the crew really knew him well. It made for a sad passage when a man was lost, but everyone knew the risks of being at sea. When the *Potter* reached port, the captain reported the lost man, sent his belongings to his next of kin and replaced him.

On other passages, there were foggy calms that left the ship drifting, with her sails slatting from one side to the other. It was during those calm passages that the mate set the crew to painting and maintaining the sails and rigging. The captain kept the men busy. There were usually some times between watches when one or more of the crew could fish off the stern with hand lines. Abram had taken Lydia's advice and spent much of his free time reading. Captain Benson subscribed to the American Seaman's Friend Society, which loaned boxes of books to ships when they visited New York. Abram read *Treasure Island* and *Twenty Thousand Leagues under the Sea*, among others. Sometimes, sailors in the fo'c'sle took to drink. The captain allowed no drinking on duty, but he didn't try to deny liquor to his men, as long as it didn't affect their work. When he or the mate noticed that a man's duties were being affected by alcohol, he was disciplined by docking his pay and having his access to liquor taken away.

Passages took anywhere from five to fourteen days, depending on the weather and how deeply the ship was loaded. They entered the ports of Baltimore, Philadelphia, New York, Bridgeport and Boston in the North and Norfolk, Wilmington, Georgetown, Charleston and Savannah in the South. They carried as cargo everything including railroad crossties, poles and pilings, lumber and barrels of rice, rosin, tar and turpentine, all going north. Going south, they carried coal, salt, iron rails, building stone and manufactured goods for hardware stores. Sometimes, the passages south would be in ballast, with the holds almost empty. In 1883, the *Warren B. Potter* loaded a cargo of more than one hundred barrels of whiskey in New York and sailed to Bermuda, where it was unloaded. Some whiskey distillers claimed a theory that the sloshing around during passages at sea contributed to the aging process, but the main reason to go to a foreign country was to avoid paying the tax.

Chapter 3

First Mate on
the *Warren B. Potter*

(1885–1892)

In 1885, after three years as a seaman, Abram Jones Slocum was made first mate of the *Potter*. Captain Benson retired and was replaced by Captain Andrews. The move from the fo'c'sle cabin to the aft cabin was a big step in any sailor's life. Instead of a hard double bunk in a compartment with three other sailors, Abram now shared the aft cabin with the captain and the engineer and had his own compartment with a bunk and more storage space for his personal belongings, including a shelf full of books he had collected. More importantly, he was in charge of the deck watches and could take over from the captain when necessary. He was now an officer, a big step up in his social status on the ship. When he had been in the fo'c'sle, the makeup of the crew had changed from passage to passage. Ordinary seamen were poorly paid, the work was hard and dangerous and not many men stuck to that kind of life any longer than they had to. Some of Abram's associates in the fo'c'sle had been alcoholics, misfits or just plain no-goods. There were a few whom he enjoyed being around, but not many. Abram had preferred to keep to himself, write to his family and read everything he could get his hands on. Abram was happy to move aft.

The *Potter* began calling more frequently at Georgetown, South Carolina. Abram had found a few friendly people in Georgetown, mostly those who worked in stores along Front Street. He had gotten to know Mr. Ehrich, Mr. Ford and Eddie Kaminski, the eldest son of Heiman Kaminski, who was owner of Kaminski Hardware and a distinguished leader of Georgetown's business community. Eddie introduced Abram to

The *Warren B. Potter* loads lumber in Georgetown, South Carolina. *Courtesy of Georgetown County Digital Library.*

Managers stand in front of the 1840 Kaminski Hardware Building. *Courtesy of Georgetown County Digital Library.*

his father. Mr. Kaminski led Abram up the stairs to his second-floor office. He told Abram that in the room where they stood, Captain Daggett had put together the exploding mine that sank the Union flagship *Harvest Moon* during the War of Northern Aggression. Abram had heard the story about the *Harvest Moon* being sunk by a floating mine in 1865 in Winyah Bay. He could see the top of the stack of the sunken ship whenever the *Potter* was towed through the bay.

On one occasion in 1885, the *Potter* was towed beyond Georgetown to where Winyah Bay branched off into the Great Pee Dee River. At its mouth, the river was wide, with salt marshes stretching away on both sides. Farther along, the river branched off again into the Black River and narrowed. The *Potter* glided silently past majestic cypress trees with smooth gray trunks, protruding knees and feathery needles. Black River was named for the dark color of the water, caused by rotting vegetation from the trees, called tannin. Farther up the river, earthen dikes of rice fields lined the river on both sides. They passed a wharf crowded with wooden barrels of rice and a sign lettered "Keithfield." As they passed a marshy bank, two big alligators—the first ones Abram had ever seen—pushed off and swam across the river. Abram saw, between the trees, tall white columns of a ruined plantation house, but he saw no people. There were a few cabins along the riverbank with black people washing their clothes and a man fishing with a cane pole. The river narrowed even more, and it was hard to see how the *Potter* could be turned around. The tug towed them beyond the wharf of Jacob Savage's lumber mill to a wider place in the river, where they were pushed against a bluff and turned around. It was a good thing that the *Potter* was almost empty because there was barely enough water to turn. The tug pushed the *Potter* against the rough lumber mill wharf, and she was tied up. They had come almost five miles up the Black River.

There, piled on the dock, were stacks of heavy curved live oak tree limbs, sawn flat on two sides. More lumber arrived in ox-drawn carts. Abram learned that the limbs were being cut from two-hundred-year-old trees scattered through the woods more than ten miles away from the wharf. Men from a shipyard in Bath, Maine, had traveled down to Savage's sawmill, bringing patterns of curved frames, knees and other parts of a ship's structure, which they needed for building two big schooners in their shipyard. They would place the drawings near a live oak tree whose major branches had the same natural curves and sizes that they needed. Black laborers then chopped down the tree and cut off the selected branches with axes and saws. They shaped them further with adzes, axes and saws until they were suitably sized

The *Warren B. Potter* at Olivet, up the Black River. *Courtesy of Maine Maritime Museum.*

to build into the ship. The live oak timbers were extremely hard and durable but difficult to cut and shape. The Maine shipyard men admitted they were having a hard time finding suitable trees because most of the big live oaks had been cut down long ago. Captain Andrews could tell that the *Potter*'s loading wouldn't be completed for several days.

When Abram awoke in the early morning, the silent river was shrouded in mist. Heavy dew covered the rails and decks of the *Potter*. Abram stood on the quarterdeck, breathing in the smells of a spring morning. An owl's hoot echoed across the water from a cypress swamp. Slowly, the sun whitened the fog and began to disperse it. The last of the mist hovered above the river's surface. Abram watched a white heron wading in the shallows across the river. He heard the clank of pots in the galley and walked forward for a cup of coffee.

Abram found some friendly southerners in this place. A small settlement had grown up around the sawmill on land that had been part of an abandoned rice plantation. The original owner had been unable to find laborers to work the rice fields after his slaves had been freed. He had given up and moved away. Jacob Savage, a Yankee, had bought the land for almost nothing and set up a sawmill operation. He built a wharf, which was used by him and nearby turpentiners, who had been poor farmers before the war and found that they could eke out a living by slashing pines and collecting rosin, tar and turpentine. Savage also provided work for independent timber cutters, who felled pine trees and had them dragged by oxen to the river and floated down the river to his sawmill. The poor little community was called Olivet. Savage had built a small general store where lumbermen, turpentiners and farmers bought their supplies and met to discuss their problems.

Abram spent some time in the store, which was run by Jacob Savage's attractive young daughter, Jane. She had lived in Olivet almost all of her life. She had a southern country accent and didn't seem to mind Yankees or sailors. When Abram told her about the alligators he had seen, she gave a gravelly laugh and said, "Honey, we got snakes and we got alligators around here, but the women are friendly." The same was true of most of the store's customers, who hadn't been slave owners and hadn't lost much as a result of the war because they hadn't had much to lose. They now had hopes that things were improving. They had never liked the planters or their families, who had pretended to be aristocrats and looked down on poor white farmers. Abram learned a lot about southern country people, and he got along well with them.

A turpentiner invited Abram to his house to meet his family and share a meal. They rowed a flat-bottomed bateau up the river and landed in front of a rough log cabin, as poor a place as Abram had ever seen. The cabin was set in a grove of pine trees. It had four small square rooms, a front stoop, a well and an outhouse. Abram met the turpentiner's plain wife and their four children; another one was on the way. They didn't have much to talk about but seemed pleased to hear Abram's stories about storms and the big cities he had visited. They dished out a meal of squirrel stew, rice and collard greens. They were generous with what little they had. A few days later, a tug arrived and the *Potter*, loaded with live oak tree limbs, lumber, cypress shingles and barrels of tar and rosin, was towed back down the dark tannic waters of the Black River toward Winyah Bay.

Throughout 1885 and 1886, the *Potter* continued to make passages from Georgetown to the Northeast and back. In May 1887, the *Potter* was tied up to a wharf at Tyson Lumber Company at the foot of Cannon Street in Georgetown. Captain Andrews called Georgetown his second home and said he would retire there one day. He liked to tie up at Tyson's because the Red Store Tavern was just across the street. The Red Store Tavern was a gathering place for the officers of schooners and steamships who visited Georgetown. It was one of the oldest establishments in Georgetown, having been built before the Revolutionary War. The Red Store was the

A painting of the schooner *Linah C. Kaminski*, 1885. *Courtesy of Mr. and Mrs. Michael Prevost.*

place where the famous Theodosia Burr Alston, daughter of Aaron Burr, had boarded the ship *Patriot* in 1812 heading for New York and was never heard from again.

One evening while the *Potter* was being loaded with lumber, Captain Andrews invited Abram to accompany him to the Red Store Tavern to have a few drinks and meet some of his friends. Captain Andrews spotted Captain Woodbury sitting at a table in the back. They greeted each other, and Captain Andrews introduced Abram to the salty captain of the three-masted schooner *Linah C. Kaminski*. Captain Andrews told Abram that the *Linah C. Kaminski* had been built by the same shipyard in Bath, the Goss and Sawyer Shipyard, as the *Warren B. Potter*, just three years after the *Potter* was built. She was owned by Heiman Kaminski and several other distinguished citizens of Georgetown, Bucksville and Conwayborough, including Captain Woodbury himself. Abram and Captain Andrews sat down at the table with Captain Woodbury with their shots of rum and beer chasers. Captain Woodbury said he had been drinking for over an hour and was not feeling so well. He had come to the Red Store Tavern after a long meeting with Heiman Kaminski in his office. He asked Captain Andrews if he had heard about his accident and was surprised that he hadn't. Captain Woodbury then began his story:

If you haven't heard by now, I guess I better tell you, so you won't hear it wrong from somebody else. Two months ago, on March 7, we sailed out of Georgetown with a cargo of naval stores for New York. We encountered bad weather almost from the beginning of the passage. About 2:00 a.m. on the third day out, while heading north-northwest under close reefed sails, our position being twenty miles off Cape Charles, an alarm signal was given by the watch that a vessel was right ahead. In less time than it takes to tell it, we and the other vessel came together head-on. The other vessel, a three-masted schooner, struck on our port bow, cutting waist and side down from fore to the mizzen rigging to below the deck, taking one wale off in places. As soon as we struck, the other schooner dropped anchor, which separated us, and a minute thereafter my main and mizzenmasts came down with a crash. I also thought the mainmast of the other schooner came down, as I heard a crash on board her also. While the two vessels were together, my crew of mates, men and steward deserted my vessel and jumped on board the other, leaving myself and my wife alone. I commanded my mate and crew to return to the Kaminski, *but they paid no attention. As soon as we separated, we drifted helplessly away to the eastward. During the whole of that day, I had a lookout for passing vessels. I saw a number of them, but not one bore down on us. One schooner passed so close that I could see the men walking on deck, and they must have seen us in our helpless condition, but they made no effort to come near. Mrs. Woodbury was painfully bruised by the force of the collision but bore up wonderfully well during the trying day and night we spent alone on the deck of the* Kaminski. *I tied Mrs. Woodbury to the spanker mast to keep her from being washed overboard. I manned the pumps as best I could through the night. The next day, on Wednesday, a German ship, the* Dakota *from Hamburg, spotted us about 6:00 a.m. and approached us. I signaled from the deck, and they hove to and sent a lifeboat near us. A heavy sea was running and a gale of wind was blowing, but they took us off. We saved nothing and were exhausted by the time we boarded the* Dakota. *Captain Schaeffer brought us into Baltimore. No man could have done more for us than he did.*

I found out later that the schooner that hit us, the Henry Withington, *was also badly damaged and was finally towed into Philadelphia by the steamship* City of Puebla. *My crew was aboard her, and I hoped never to see those bastards again. The wrecked but still floating* Kaminski *was found by a fishing smack, which towed her into Sandy Hook and claimed her as a prize. The fishing boat crew claimed they were going to have her repaired and use her themselves. I'm in a hell of a mess.*

I spent all day today trying to explain to Heiman Kaminski why it happened. The Linah C. Kaminski *is named after his mother, you know. He's very upset. We're filing a lawsuit against the owners of the* Henry Withington *for running into us. They were at fault, but I'll probably never get my crew to testify. They've disappeared. Our owners' agent, H.H. Grant, is trying to reason with the agent for the fishing boat to regain possession of the* Kaminski. *We'll probably have to pay plenty for that to happen. And then there's the cost of the repairs. I'm in trouble, as you can see. I don't know what I'm going to do.*

"I think you need another drink," said Captain Andrews. Abram and Captain Andrews stayed with Captain Woodbury for another hour and finally convinced him to go back to his lodging. He was supposed to return the following day to Conwayborough, where he and his wife owned a house. Abram and Captain Andrews returned to the *Potter*. Abram hoped he would never be faced with a situation like the one Captain Woodbury was in.

Later in 1887, the *Potter* delivered a load of lumber to Bridgeport, Connecticut, and was due to go into a shipyard there to have her hull checked, scraped and painted. Abram would have a week off. He wanted to go home to Cuttyhunk to visit his family. Captain Andrews paid off the crew and said he wanted to treat them to a couple rounds of drinks at his favorite Bridgeport bar. The Bridgeport waterfront was a typical sleazy several blocks of bars and burlesque houses, with a few prostitutes roaming the area. Captain Andrews's selection was about the best of the lot, with a gaudy front entrance, a long bar, plenty of tables and a stage for the girly show. The place was crowded on a Friday night, with lots of noise. Abram could easily see that most of the clientele were sailors from the many steam and sailing ships that arrived and departed from Bridgeport on a regular basis. Captain Andrews was generous and stood two rounds. There were toasts to the ship, some off-key singing and a few dirty stories before the captain excused himself to go back to the ship.

Abram had just enough time to catch the last train to New Bedford. He had been with the crew of the *Potter* constantly for the past year or more, and he was ready to get away from them. He barely caught the last train and knew he would have to find a boat to take him to Cuttyhunk. Abram spotted a steam launch that belonged to a Cuttyhunk neighbor. He found the owner and hitched a ride back to the island. His family was surprised and happy to see him. His sister, Myra, had never married and was still living with Lydia and helping at the school. Frederick Jr. was twelve years old and, according to Lydia, was a brilliant student of science. Still, Frederick looked up to his older brother and wanted to hear all about his adventures. Abram was distressed to see his father in failing health. He was sixty-seven but looked much older. Lydia took Abram aside and told him that her husband had been very sick. It would be impossible for them to remain on the island, and they were going to move into a house on the mainland at Fairhaven. Abram spent most of his time with his father, knowing that this might be the last time he would see him. Abram rode back to New Bedford in the launch with Myra and Frederick Jr. Then he rejoined the ship, loaded coal for Charleston and sailed.

Charleston had once been the busiest and most prosperous port city on the southeastern coast. However, by 1887, the city was in desolation and the port in a dilapidated condition. A fire in 1861 had burned much of the downtown area, the Union bombardment during the Civil War had further wrecked the city and the recent earthquake of 1886 had toppled buildings and caused more destruction. Many of the old piers had rotted or been destroyed by storms. Still, many ships visited Charleston to load cotton and lumber products and to bring supplies into the city. A coal pier had been repaired, and the *Potter* was able to unload her cargo. Abram was happy to get away from the Holy City—the city that had started the war.

Four months later, Abram received a telegram in Savannah saying that his father had died. He managed to get time off to be with his family. He rode a train for thirty hours to Fairhaven and spent a few days with Lydia, Myra, Edward and Frederick. They were settled into a pleasant house, and he could see that they would be fine when they got over their grief. Abram found out from Lydia that his father had willed his interest in the *Warren B. Potter* to him. Before he returned to his ship, Abram told Lydia that he intended to marry a girl in New Bedford that he had been courting for a year.

It was a cold day in late February 1888 when the *Potter* left Georgetown loaded with 250,000 feet of lumber. The first day out was uneventful, with a moderate east wind and help from the Gulf Stream. That night, the wind shifted to the northeast. When the *Potter* was within thirty miles of Cape Hatteras, the northeast wind grew stronger and the barometer began falling. It became overcast and started to rain. The wind increased gradually in force but remained steady from the northeast until 11:00

a.m., when it shifted suddenly to west-northwest, throwing everything back. Captain Andrews had already reduced sail, expecting heavy weather, as the barometer had been falling all day and the wind increasing. In a few minutes the wind hauled to the northwest. The sky was overcast and black overhead, so dark that they couldn't make out the clouds. There was occasional lightning and heavy thunder. The seas were high from the southeast. They began to break onboard and do considerable damage. Two of the chains holding the starboard deck load of lumber parted, and boards were flying all over the ship, many of them overboard. The lowest barometer reading was 29.4. By nightfall, the *Potter's* position was about twenty miles east by south from Cape Henry.

All the crew had been on deck and busy for more than twenty-four hours. There were two men at the wheel trying to keep the pitching, rolling ship heading toward Cape Henry and the safety of Norfolk. Abram and two other men wrestled the flogging shreds of a jib that had broken loose from the jib boom. The engineer was braced against a bulkhead in the forward cabin, feeding coal into the furnace that heated steam for the donkey engine. The cook held on to the doorway of the galley, having given up on heating water for coffee. Captain Andrews stared grimly ahead, hoping to see Cape Henry Light.

When Abram returned to a slight shelter from the wind behind the forward cabin, he felt he was in his world—the world he loved, the excitement, the adventure, even the fury of the sea and danger of death. He leaned out from around the lee side of the fo'c'sle cabin and faced forward, into the wind. As the ship rose on a wave, he thought he saw a flash. He craned his neck and squinted into the stinging rain. There it was again. It was a flash. It had to be Cape Henry Light. He yelled in the direction of Captain Andrews. He crawled back across the lumber piles, holding on to a rope they had stretched along the rigging for safety. He reached Captain Andrews. By that time, he had seen it too.

By morning, they had both anchors down, still pitching but safe in the harbor. It was very cold and snowing hard. The barometer had begun to rise, and the wind was lessening. At noon, the pilot's launch steamed alongside, and the pilot was able to grab the Jacob's ladder and climb aboard. He told them how lucky they were. News from the telegraph had told of the worst winter storm of the century. Many ships were aground or missing between New York and Boston. Many lives would be lost.

Later in the afternoon, the *Potter* was towed to a pier in the shipyard to await better weather for repairs. She had shredded some sails, lost one topmast, splintered timbers along her starboard rail and lost the ship's yawl, which had been hung from davits at the stern. Three of the crew decided to leave the ship permanently. Captain Andrews paid them off, with pay docked for not completing the passage. The others, including Abram, were given unpaid leave for a week, awaiting repairs. Captain Andrews reported to his agent in New York, saying they were safe but would be at least two weeks late on delivery of cargo.

For the next five years, Abram Slocum was mate on the *Warren B. Potter*, serving under Captain Andrews. The *Potter* made regular passages from Georgetown and Savannah to Baltimore, Philadelphia, New York, Bridgeport and Boston, hauling mostly lumber on northern passages and miscellaneous cargo or ballast on southern passages. Depending on the time of year, these passages lasted anywhere from six days to three weeks. Abram had married in 1888. In 1889, while Abram was at sea, his young wife died after delivering a healthy baby girl. The baby, named Florence after her mother, lived with Lydia and Myra in Fairhaven. Abram's brother Frederick finished at the top of his high school class in Fairhaven and earned a scholarship to Brown University.

Chapter 4

MASTER OF THE THREE-MASTED
SCHOONER *WARREN B. POTTER*

(1892–1901)

In 1892, Captain Andrews decided to retire. He recommended to the other owners of the *Potter* that Abram Jones Slocum be made captain. There were no objections. The last voyage of the two captains together ended in Georgetown, South Carolina, where Captain Andrews had decided to live in retirement. He had never married. The two captains docked the *Potter* at the Tyson Lumber Company wharf, paid off the crew, made sure that everything was shipshape, secured the *Potter* and walked over to the Red Store Tavern. They had a few beers together, reminisced about voyages aboard the *Potter*, toasted their change of command and parted.

Abram Slocum had his first command. He walked back to the *Potter*. He examined each foot of her, from the carved and slightly battered wooden figurehead of Mr. Warren Potter to the ship's yawl hanging from davits at the stern and needing a paint job. He climbed onboard and turned a key in the lock of the starboard door to the aft cabin—his cabin. Captain Andrews had removed all of his gear. He had sold Abram his sextant, which was better than the old one his father had given him many years ago. The charts belonged with the ship. He opened the chart drawer and pulled out a stack of coastal charts, showing inlets and harbors from as far north as the coast of Maine to as far south as the island of Trinidad. They were all neatly folded and marked with the latest changes. He put them away. He sat on his bed, the only bed on the ship. It was screwed to the floor and had a removable bunk board to keep him from rolling out. It needed a new mattress and pillow. He crossed over to the mate's cabin, carried his clothing and other gear to the captain's cabin and put everything away. He carefully arranged the books he had collected. He would have to have more shelving built. He sat at the desk where the ship's log lay. He turned to the last entry, dipped his pen in the ink and wrote, "Change of Command ceremony. Captain John Andrews relieved by Captain Abram Jones Slocum." Abram felt the power of being the ship's captain, commanding his own floating kingdom. At that moment, he was a proud man.

Abram had invited George Pierson, a friend and experienced mate from another schooner, to be first mate on the *Potter*, and he had accepted. Abram kept both the engineer and the cook, a black man from South Carolina. He would have to find four able seamen. He knew of a Norwegian fisherman who lived in Georgetown who was a good bosun and might be convinced to sign on the *Potter*. The others he would have to find in the bars along Georgetown's waterfront.

Tyson Lumber Company's stevedores loaded the *Potter* with beams and boards. Captain Slocum had found a crew, although of questionable ability. He set the men to doing maintenance of the ship. He bought a new mattress at Kaminski Hardware. He went into a barbershop and had his beard shaved off. Now that he had his first command, he felt a need to start clean shaven. He had the ship stocked with food and supplies from C.L. Ford, Ship Chandlery. His crew sealed the lumber ports in the bow and chained down the deck lumber. He contacted the *Congdon* tug captain, whom he knew well. He contacted the port pilot and prepared to get underway. He posted a letter to Lydia. The lines were cast off, and the *Congdon* towed the *Potter* down the Sampit River to Winyah Bay and through the bay, past the lighthouse and across the bar into the Atlantic. Captain Slocum ordered the foresail, mainsail and spanker hoisted by the donkey engine, and the crew ran out two jibs. The wind was right for setting topsails. They sailed north-northeast on a starboard tack, making eight knots, heading toward the Gulf Stream. The *Potter* arrived in New York six days after departing from Georgetown, a good first passage for Captain Slocum. The lumber cargo was unloaded in Brooklyn after a two-day wait. The New York agent for the *Potter* arranged for the schooner to load railroad rails in New York to be delivered to Georgetown. The federal government had approved the construction of stone jetties for a new and deeper entrance to Winyah Bay. The rails were to be used to build a track from the main line to the edge of the Sampit River so that construction materials and stone could be loaded onto barges.

The *Potter* arrived in Georgetown the day after Christmas after a lucky storm-free December passage. The rails were unloaded, and the *Potter* was towed up the Black River to load lumber at Jacob Savage's mill. There would be a delay because the boiler that supplied steam to the sawmill had exploded and was being repaired. There was no passenger train from Georgetown to the main north–south railroad line, so Abram would have to spend January 1893 tied up to the wharf in Olivet.

Abram enjoyed an Olivet New Year's Eve celebration, which included dancing to banjo and fiddle music and the eating of a hog, cooked for a long time on a spit over hickory logs. The State of South Carolina had started dispensing liquor in its own bottles to collect the tax, so the citizens of Olivet made white lightning and dispensed plenty of whiskey without tax. Abram found himself respected and almost famous as a ship captain in the community of Olivet. He had begun to feel at home in the Deep South.

On one beautiful cool clear day in January, Jane Savage knocked on the door of Abram's aft cabin and said that she wanted to introduce him to friends of hers. Standing on the wharf were a couple who looked to be in their sixties. He was a tall, distinguished gentleman with white hair. She must have been a beautiful woman when she was younger. She was well dressed, as if she had just come from church. They were introduced as Oliver and Mary Smith. They spoke as educated people, he with an almost British accent and she with a slight southern drawl. They had wanted to meet the captain because they understood that he appreciated literature. They said they had some books he might be interested in if he would be willing to trade some of his. Abram invited them to come aboard. He showed them the shelves of books in his cabin, and they both saw ones that they might like to borrow or trade. They invited Abram to come to their home for tea that afternoon and drove away in their buggy.

Jane told Abram that Oliver Smith had been owner of Lark Hill Plantation before the Civil War. His family had lived there for generations and had been aristocratic rice planters with many slaves. He had fought in the war, and Mary had stayed behind to try to keep the plantation going. Just at the end of the war, her slaves ran away, and she wasn't able to harvest the rice crop. After the war, some freed slaves had raided her house and taken many valuable things. When Oliver Smith returned, they had no money, and he lost the plantation for unpaid taxes. Jane's father had bought the plantation for almost nothing and moved down from Pennsylvania to start the sawmill. Jane said that Oliver and Mary lived a few miles away, where he and some helpers tried to make a living from farming pine trees for naval stores. Jane told Abram how to find their house and loaned Abram a horse.

Abram had no trouble finding the house. It was one story with whitewashed cypress clapboards and was set back from the river in a clearing shaded by a big live oak. Oliver Smith greeted Abram, and they sat on a porch looking out toward the river. Abram learned that Oliver had graduated from West Point long before the beginning of the Civil War. He had joined Lee's army and served in Virginia for most of the war. Abram told Oliver about his childhood aboard his father's whaler during the Civil War years. While they were talking, a black man approached the porch and asked Oliver if he could come look at the turpentine still, which wasn't working. Oliver asked Abram if he would like to come with him. They climbed into a wagon and drove through a forest of longleaf pine trees for about a mile to a shed in a clearing. Three other black men were standing next to the shed waiting for the turpentine still to be fixed. After Oliver told them what had to be done to make it work, he led Abram into the forest to show him his naval stores operation.

Many of the longleaf pine trees close to the turpentine shed were dead. Some had been cut down, and only their stumps remained. They were mostly eighteen to twenty-four inches in diameter. A trough had been cut out of each tree near the base of the tree. The troughs were called boxes. Above the boxes were a series of deep gouges in the face of the tree, one above the other, where the sap or resin had run down the face of the tree and into one of the boxes. These particular trees had been used up, and there were so many gouges in the trees that they had died. Farther along were trees that were still being used to collect resin in their boxes. Nothing was going on during the winter because sap wouldn't start to flow down from the gouges until it was warm in the spring. Then, Oliver said, laborers would collect resin from the boxes with ladles and bring barrels of resin to the still. He said that farther into the woods, laborers were cutting new boxes in the bases of trees that hadn't been tapped previously.

They walked back to the still, and Oliver showed Abram how the resin was boiled and turpentine was distilled in a copper still and poured into wooden barrels, which were made by skilled laborers during the winter. At the bottom of the still were valves where the residue (rosin) was drained off. Rosin was poured into other barrels and shipped to factories in the North that made ink, soap and other products. Oliver guessed that the next time Abram brought the *Potter* to Olivet, it would be to load turpentine and rosin. Oliver said he made a bare living from his production of naval stores. His laborers made so little that they had to cut timber and sharecrop for Jacob Savage to put food on their tables. Oliver said that he had previously made tar and pitch, but it didn't pay anymore. He showed Abram an old tar pit where resinous pieces of pine had been burned slowly so that the resin melted, formed tar and flowed to a low point in the pit. The tar had been drawn off and ladled into barrels. Some of the tar had been boiled to produce pitch. Abram knew the smells of tar and pitch from his days of sailing on his father's whaler.

Oliver said that longleaf pine trees for producing naval stores were very scarce. Suitable trees that hadn't already been used up or cut down for lumber could be found in only the remotest parts of the country. Some trees had burned in forest fires, been blown down by hurricanes or died from disease. A longleaf pine took over fifty years to mature to a suitable size for naval stores, and no new trees were being planted. It wouldn't be long, he guessed, before the naval stores industry would be dead.

They rode back to Oliver's house for tea. Mary Smith greeted Abram at the door to their parlor. The room was not large and was filled by a few pieces of fine furniture and mementoes from the house they had owned before the Civil War. Their old plantation house had burned before Jacob Savage had bought the plantation property. Abram was particularly fascinated by a wall of bookshelves containing leather-bound volumes by nineteenth-century authors whose names he recognized. The three of them sat at an elegant dining room table as Mary poured tea from a silver service that had been in her family for three generations. They sat and talked about old times. Abram asked Mary how she managed while her husband was fighting in the war. She smiled and told a story:

It was in the summer of 1863 when a Yankee steamboat came up the river and stopped in front of our house. The boat anchored, and some Union sailors rowed over to our dock. Except for my house slaves, I was by myself. Some of our field hands ran down to the dock, hoping to get their freedom on that Yankee boat. One of the worst of my hands led those sailors to the cooling house in the side yard, where the Christmas wine was stored. They broke open the door, took the wine and began to drink some pretty good French wine out of the bottles. I stayed inside, looking out of a window, but it wasn't long before those drunken sailors walked across my yard and up on my porch. I didn't have time to find the pistol Oliver had given me, but I went to the front door anyway and told them to go away. One of them, the drunkest of the lot, demanded I give him all the money in the house. I stood up as tall as I could and told him just what I thought of him. I gave him a verbal lashing he wouldn't forget, although I was scared to death. I think I surprised him, and he didn't know what to do. Then, I did the thing that saved me. I started to cry. I couldn't help it. One of the other sailors pulled out a handkerchief, handed it to me and said, "Don't cry, lady, we won't do you no harm." Well, they took their wine and went back to their boat. Three of my slaves went with them, but I didn't care. They turned that steamboat around and headed back toward Georgetown. I was shaking like a leaf but was proud about what I had done. My house slaves were proud of me too. That was my most exciting story of the war.

"She was a real tiger," Oliver exclaimed. "It's a wonder that you Yankees won the war."

"I surely didn't have anything to do with it," said Abram. "With women as brave as you, I'm surprised, too."

At the end of the afternoon, Abram returned to his ship with a book of poetry by Henry Timrod, who, Oliver told him, was the poet of the Confederacy. Abram promised to give the Smiths any books they wanted from the *Potter*.

The sawmill boiler had been repaired and cutting of lumber for delivery to Philadelphia had been completed. The *Potter* was towed down Black River, through Winyah Bay and into the Atlantic on January 22, 1893, heading for Philadelphia. The weather was bitter cold with a twenty-five-knot wind out of the northwest. They sailed, close hauled on a port tack, up the coast, bashing through steep, choppy waves of the Gulf Stream. The *Potter* passed well east of Cape Hatteras and continued northeast for another day before tacking to the west, toward the Delaware Breakwater, a harbor of refuge at the mouth of Delaware Bay. The temperature was below twenty degrees, but facing into the wind, it felt like below zero. As the *Potter* approached Cape May on January 26, Abram saw the sails of many other ships wallowing back and forth near the red lighthouse that marked the entrance to the Delaware Breakwater. He discovered that the entrance into Delaware Bay was blocked by ice. Icebreaker steam tugs were working to clear it. Finally, in the late afternoon of January 28, the entrance was cleared of ice, and nineteen vessels were able to pass into the bay. The *Potter* and her almost-frozen crew tied up to a pier in Philadelphia on the morning of January 29.

During the remainder of 1893, the *Potter* made several passages to New Haven, loaded with lumber from Georgetown or Darien, Georgia. On April 6, 1894, the *Warren B. Potter*, commanded by Captain Slocum, left Georgetown heading for New York City with a cargo of 300,000 feet of lumber. The weather deteriorated almost at once. The *Potter* passed outside of Cape Hatteras in high winds and heavy seas and was forced to shelter behind the Delaware Breakwater to await a break in the weather. On the night of April 9, Captain Slocum set sail from behind the Delaware Breakwater, but soon after the *Potter* got out to sea, she encountered a storm. It was only a small blow when she departed, but a few miles out, the wind blew with hurricane force.

The *Potter* rolled and tossed in the seas, and great volumes of water came over the deck, sweeping off part of the deck load. First Mate George Pierson was moving about the deck when a monster wave boarded the vessel. It struck him like a shot from a cannon, and he was knocked down and nearly washed overboard. He was fortunate, however, and he was found between the fo'c'sle and the deck load of lumber. Pierson was badly bruised and his left ankle sprained. The *Potter* was still but a few miles from shore, so Captain Slocum headed the vessel out to sea. They were swept 150 miles offshore before turning back toward New York.

As the *Potter* battled back toward shore, on April 15, the schooner *Helen J. Holway* of Machiasport, Maine, was spotted by Captain Slocum fifty miles off Cape May, New Jersey, waterlogged and in a sinking condition. Despite strong winds and high seas, the crew of the *Potter* managed to take the crew of the *Holway*—six men—off the sinking schooner and onto the *Potter*. The crew of the *Holway* had manned pumps for over thirty-six hours before they gave up in exhaustion. Signals of distress had been sent, and the *Potter* had responded. The *Potter* brought up at Sandy Hook on April 16, leaving the crew of the *Holway* there. The *Holway* had been bound from New York for Brookline, Maine. Later, a tug towed the *Potter* to a wharf in New York City to unload her cargo.

Abram had no chance to visit Lydia and Florence in Fairhaven. The agent in New York wanted the *Potter* to load more iron rails for Georgetown and go back to Olivet for lumber and naval stores. Abram and the *Potter* had a much easier passage south with a steady east wind. The night skies were clear, filled with millions of stars and a waxing half moon. One night, he stood watch on the quarterdeck from eight o'clock until midnight, feeling the breeze on his face and knowing that this was the only life for him. He was relieved at midnight by George Pierson, who had recovered from his sprained ankle.

After the iron rails were unloaded at the government wharf in Georgetown, a tug towed the *Potter* along a familiar route up the Black River to Jacob Savage's wharf at Olivet. The *Potter* was squeezed in between two other schooners, the *Thomas Winsmore* and the *B.I. Hazard*, both there to load lumber. Almost immediately, Jacob Savage and Jane Savage came aboard and asked Abram for the use of the deck of the *Warren B. Potter* for a full-moon, May Day party and dance to be held that coming weekend. The *Potter* was the only one of the three schooners that was not already partially loaded with lumber. Abram agreed to their request and put his crew to work to make the weekend a success. The following Monday, an article about the weekend appeared in the *Georgetown Times*:

Pleasant Times at Olivet

Olivet, May 7 1894
To the Editor of The Times:
The week ending Sunday, the 6ᵗʰ, has been one of the most eventful in the history of this place. At present we can hardly call this settlement more than a "place" but we are in hopes to soon see it incorporated as a town or city. Considering the size of Olivet, it cannot be equaled for business or pleasure. Three schooners have been loading at the wharf for Northern ports, viz: the Thomas Winsmore, *Capt J. Conwell, of Philadelphia; the* B.I. Hazard, *Capt Rafford, of New York; and the* Warren B. Potter, *Capt Slocum, of New Bedford. More vessels have loaded at this wharf the past six months than any other one mill in the vicinity of Georgetown. When the saw is buzzing and the vessels coming and going, how can Mr. Savage and his assistants be otherwise than happy?*

To vary the monotony of the regular routine of saw-mill life, the young people are to be thanked for their energy in furnishing amusements of different kinds for the inhabitants. Last Wednesday evening we all enjoyed a pleasant and social time with Mrs. Green and family at her residence, "River Side Cottage." Dancing was the principal amusement of the evening, followed by a collation of cake, cream and lemonade, which was enjoyed by all present. The event proved such a success that the committee on "good times" took a unanimous vote to have the dance repeated on Friday eve, and selected the deck of the schooner W.B. Potter *as the most suitable place. The captain was immediately notified and the crew was soon at work. The main deck from the main-mast to the taffrail was covered with awnings, and the sides enclosed with flags. The interior was decorated with the bunting from the three schooners and illuminated with red, white and green lights; and after waxing the floor, we had a ball-room that Georgetown might be envious of. The ball began to roll at 9 PM, and was on the move until 1 AM, Saturday morning. Music was furnished by Mr. Rooney (a near relative of Annie's) a musician of very high merit, being a skillful manipulator of the violin, banjo and accordian. The crowd was very ably handled by the notorious and illustrious P.J. Doyle, assisted by Mr. Fred Broomer and the officers of the schooner. If appearances tend to show anything, everyone enjoyed the evening very much, and at 1:30 AM, all agreed that rackets "on the river" are hard to beat, and picked their way homeward through the piles of lumber, sawdust and slabs. Too much cannot be said in praise of the gallant captain who used such Herculean efforts to get the schooner in order and who was untiring in his efforts to make all feel at home and spend a pleasant evening. The captain's coming is always looked forward to with pleasant anticipation by Olivetians in general and the hammock fastenings are examined closely, and he always enjoys the freedom of the city. We noticed among the visitors, Capt Conwell and wife of schooner* Thomas Winsmore, *Capt Rafford, of sch.* B.I. Hazard; *Miss Mattie Jeanerette, and Jas. Carraway, of Georgetown.*

Miss Mattie Jeanerette has returned to her home in Georgetown, after spending a few weeks with her friend, Miss E. Green. Boat rides on the river and moonlight serenades will be missed by the Olivet dudes.

Abram enjoyed the weekend as much as anyone, although some of the men in the crews of the three schooners had made fools of themselves, as sailors do, with way too much to drink. The *Potter*'s drunken bosun and the tipsy Miss Mattie Jeanerette of Georgetown had rowed the ship's yawl down the river and out of sight, singing sea shanties at the top of their lungs, and they hadn't returned until after 4:00 a.m. By Tuesday, the ship was in order and lumber was being loaded.

The *Potter* made two round trips from New York to Savannah during the last months of 1894, but Abram had no opportunity to visit Georgetown. Finally, in early December, Abram and the *Potter* made a rough passage in ballast from New York to the coast off Georgetown, where they were met by the pilot boat and a steam tug, which had been alerted by the North Island lighthouse keeper's telegraph. They were towed up Winyah Bay and the

Sampit River to an anchorage off Palmetto Lumber Company, where they were to be loaded from lighters with railroad crossties.

Abram spent most evenings in the Red Store Tavern, swapping yarns with the other officers of the visiting ships. He was well liked and had become known as the intellectual captain because of his knowledge of literature. He and several of the other officers were natives of the New Bedford area and descendants of whalers. They were surprised about how little the Georgetown people knew or cared about New Bedford, even though several of their schooners were registered there and showed "New Bedford" on their sterns. Over a few rums, the other captains convinced Abram that he should write a history of New Bedford and ask Mr. Doar to print it in the Georgetown newspaper. Abram agreed to give it a try.

Over the next few weeks, he completed the proposed article. Arriving at Tyson Lumber on his next visit to Georgetown, Abram was pleased with himself as he walked up Front Street and presented the inked manuscript to Mr. Doar, editor of the *Georgetown Semi-Weekly Times*. Doar was surprised to see such an apparently well-written article presented to him by one of the sea captains, who were not known for their literary prowess. Doar asked Abram to confirm that it was he who had actually written it. Abram felt a little insulted by Doar's questioning because Doar's newspaper was no *New York Times*. In fact, Doar usually filled over half of his twice-weekly, four-page editions with criticisms and put-downs of the black people of Georgetown. It was really no honor to have an article accepted. Doar told Abram that because A.J. Slocum was a well-known and respected captain whose schooner had sailed regularly into and out of Georgetown for several years, he would agree to print Slocum's article. It appeared in the December 15, 1894 issue of the *Times*.

THE WHALE FISHERIES
Account of the Industry at New Bedford
An Interesting Article on the Subject From the Pen of our Sea Captains

To the Editor of the Times:

The stories that excite wonder and fire the imagination are those that deal with experiences far away from the common things of life. Near by affairs, on the farm, in the school, in the town or village, simply because they are familiar, thereby become common-place, and excite no curiosity; but even very simple narratives about places, peoples or ways of doing things at a distance have a fascination for every one of us and can always find eager and attentive listeners.

There has always been a sort of weird charm about tales of the sea. "They that go down to the sea in ships, that do business in great waters; these see the works of the Lord and his wonders in the deep." No words can express better than these the universal attitudes of mind to all that pertains to the wide waste of waters.

By how many cozy firesides, in lonely farmhouses, in village homes, in city dwellings, have sea faring adventures of friends and relatives been discussed; with what all absorbed interest have the hearers followed the details of the narrative, especially if the narrator had himself been a participant and possessed the sailor's usual gift of "spinning a yarn."

In the common life of New England, because of this natural interest that every one feels in maritime affairs, New Bedford has always cut a much larger figure and has been much more widely known than other places of equal population and business.

The young men from the remote farms, the rugged hillsides, the inland towns or cities, moved by a desire to see something of the world and its wonders, made their way to the wharves of the whaling city "or Blubber Town," as it was sometimes called, and from thence set forth on their quest after adventure and fortune. That they did not always realize either, in the manner or in the degree that fancy led them to expect, did not prevent others from following in their footsteps. But the experience they did achieve, although perhaps somewhat severe to most of those who ventured, still had elements of romance, especially when viewed, seated in a pleasant home, through the haze of memory. Scarcely a place in the limits of the Atlantic seaboard but furnished, one or two generations ago, some adventurous son who either went by consent or ran away to New Bedford and shipped on a whaler. That this does not happen today is mainly because of the decline of the whole fishery, but previous to the war of the Rebellion it was common, and by this means New Bedford became known far and wide. In how many books of biography and newspaper obituaries are accounts even now found of men who began life by shipping from the old whaling ports.

The main thing in the history of New Bedford has been the whale fishery. Her sons developed this business to its greatest perfection, and by its means secured the wealth that now enables them to conduct successfully the great manufacturing interest to which the city has devoted her attention since the decline of the whale industry. In the year 1750 stately woods covered the present site of the city, but Joseph Russell then had a try works on the shore, at or near the foot of Union street, and fished for whales in a primitive way off shore. A few years after, in 1765, Joseph Rotch, a Quaker from Wantucket, came to the place and also engaged in the whale fishery, introducing better methods than those Mr. Russell had employed.

At first it was only necessary to send the vessels, which were small, a short distance out to sea; gradually the game went further and further away until what was an undertaking of a few days or weeks, necessitated a voyage of months or years, and the staunch ships of New Bedford penetrated into every sea. They went into the ice fields of the North, they rounded Cape Horn and the Cape of Good Hope into the Pacific and Indian Ocean, they went into far southern latitudes and in fact into every remote region of the globe, being in many cases the pioneers in explorations and the first comers and most adventurous sailors. Little by little the business developed. The place had admirable advantages as a port—a lengthy waterfront, deep water up to the wharves, and commodious harbor, easily assessable at all conditions of wind and tide.

With all these favoring elements New Bedford ultimately absorbed nearly all the whaling business on the Atlantic seaboard, until in 1857 the fleet consisted of 450 vessels, worth more than $13,000,000 and requiring the services of over 11,000 men. In the decade from 1850 to 1860 the business was at its heights, and New Bedford with an average of a whaleship arriving every day in the year was a roistering seaport whose life and character can hardly be realized by the sedate inhabitants of the present day. In the fall months as many as ten ships would frequently be entered at the custom house in one day from all parts of the globe, but during the winter very few arrived. The traditions of those years depict the town as a very lively place, with all the elements in motion that go to make a great seaport, a picture of which can nowadays, in this age of steam and changed methods, only be imagined or instructed by the recollections of some of the old sailors of that period.

About 1857 the business began to decline but New Bedford has always maintained her relative position as the chief whaling port in the country. Two main causes, which worked together, contributed to this decline. These were the increasing scarcity of whales from year to year, necessitating voyages into more remote seas at a largely increased cost, and the discovery of petroleum, the use of which supplanted whale oil for many purposes. The cost of securing whale oil was thus increased, while its price in market was lowered, with the necessary result that capital found it unprofitable to continue in the whale fishery. This movement was checked by a fortunate rise in the price of whale bone which increased in market value seven or eight times its former figures, while the price of oil was cut into with a tendency still downward. By this means the decline of the business has been checked, but at present the number of vessels in active service is not more than an eighth or tenth of those that were fitted out in the heyday of the business. The din of the hammers of the carpenters and caulkers is however still heard on the wharves of the city and although she is shorn of her old glory as a whaling port, she has more than made up for the loss in that line by the increase of her merchant ships and phenomenal growth of her manufactures, so that at present she is in the front rank as a textile manufacturing center, and has besides many other important industries.

The wharves are not such busy places as they were in the zenith of the whale fishery, but the growing manufacturing interest have brought an annually increasing life to them. Many of the best places are yet reserved for the whale ships. A number of them are always in port and they present a dismantled appearance unless they have just arrived or are ready to sail. Their presence in the commodious docks add much to the picturesque character of the waterfront, while the quantities of oil stored on some of the wide wharves in strong barrels covered with a matting of seaweed, impart a flavor of the sea to the scene.

New Bedford whale men have now changed their headquarters to San Francisco, on the Pacific, where a fleet of about 60 vessels are engaged in the Arctic whaling, catching the "right whale," principally for the bone.

These vessels are mostly large, staunch barque rigged steamers built expressly for heavy work in the ice, and many are fitted to spend the long, dark winters in the Arctic and are often away from home two or three years, being supplied by tenders from San Francisco every season.

Last winter 12 steamers and sailing ships were in winter quarters at the mouth of the Makenza River, and the sufferings and privations endured by these hardy sailors is sometimes beyond description.

The success of these Arctic cruises are varied, some making good catches, while others come home without having taken a single whale. New Bedford today is second only to Fall River in the cotton manufacturing and is steadily increasing. The first cotton mill, "The Wamsutta," was built in 1847 and the wamsutta cloth now has a worldwide reputation.

This mill has been enlarged many times and today is one of the largest in the United States.

The increase in manufacturing has caused a great demand for coal, and at any time can now be seen some of the largest four-masted schooners and barges discharging at the railroad wharfs. More coal is shipped inland from there than any other port except Providence west of Cape Cod. Some of the largest and finest merchant ships launched from the yards in the State of Maine hail from New Bedford and she also claims a good share of the coasting fleet; some of the small ones are often seen in this harbor.

A.J. Slocum
New Bedford, Mass.

Abram bought three copies of the newspaper and read and reread the article, pleased that no serious typographical errors had been made. As he walked along Front Street on Friday, purchasing various items for the *Potter,* several citizens stopped and complimented him about the article. Even Mayor Morgan, who had paid little attention to Abram before, shook his hand, praised the article and declared that they would have to have lunch together at the Palmetto Club someday soon. Abram had never noticed that Mayor Morgan had only one arm.

The next Saturday night, Abram was sitting at the bar in the Red Store Tavern, receiving praise from the other captains for his article, when they were startled by a loud voice from behind them. "Gentlemen, gentlemen, I have an announcement to make!" Abram turned and looked across the room at Moby Dick, one of Georgetown's most familiar and outrageous waterfront characters, standing just inside the front door shouting at everyone in the barroom. He was a tall, thin man with a wispy white beard that reached halfway down to his rope belt. He was wearing the same striped stocking cap that he always wore. One scrawny tattooed arm pointed toward the ceiling, as if he were getting ready to give a pronouncement from God.

I have received reliable information today from the Honorable William Buck that the famous ship Henrietta, *the largest ship ever built in the state of South Carolina, is no more. After twenty years of sailing all over the world, she has been blown ashore and wrecked by a typhoon in Kobe, Japan. I am saddened by this event, and you should be also. In case you don't know it, I was chief rigger of the* Henrietta *in '75. If anyone wants to buy me a drink, I'll tell them the whole story of the* Henrietta *and my involvement in her construction and launching.*

A sketch of the *Henrietta* under construction at Bucksville, South Carolina, 1875. *Courtesy of Penobscot Marine Museum.*

Some had heard this story before, but there was sufficient interest within the bar to hear it again. Moby Dick was seated at the head table with a large glass of rum in front of him. Moby Dick had been around Georgetown's waterfront for about as long as anyone could remember. He was an intelligent fellow and had gotten his name by reading long passages from Herman Melville's book in bars aloud. He lived on a derelict sailboat anchored in the river and worked as a sometimes fisherman and handyman at McDonald's Fish House. One thing that everyone knew he could do well was splice rope and cable. When anyone needed a cable spliced before three o'clock in the afternoon, they called on Moby Dick. If it was after three o'clock, chances were that he would be unable to undertake such a task. Abram had not heard the story of the *Henrietta*, so he turned around and listened. Moby Dick continued in his Maine accent:

> *After us Yankees whipped you Rebels in '65, some of us fellows from Searsport, Maine, were talked into coming south to build a ship for Mr. William Buck, whose family had come from Bucksport, Maine, in 1820 and settled up the Waccamaw River to cut timber and send*

it back to Maine to build ships. Well, the Buck family that founded Bucksville, South Carolina, got it in their heads that they could build ships cheaper in South Carolina than they could be built in Maine, since the lumber for the ship was in South Carolina anyway. Henry Buck built a couple of small coastal schooners in South Carolina that worked out okay, so he decided to build a big one, one that could haul cargo all over the world. He came up to Searsport in 1873 to see his friend Jonathan Nichols, the finest ship builder in Maine. Jonathan said he was willing to invest in a big ship, but he convinced Buck that there weren't no South Carolina men who had the skill to build such a ship. The only way it could be done was for the skilled shipwrights and mechanics to travel down from Searsport to South Carolina and build it.

Moby Dick stopped and took a big swig of rum. He continued:

Jonathan said it would take a hundred of us to build the ship they wanted to build. It was to be a square-rigged Down Easter, 210 feet long, 29 feet wide and 24 feet deep, 1,200 tons. That's big, the biggest ship ever built in South Carolina. Buck complained that one hundred was a lot of men, but he agreed to put us up for as long as it took. He sent his ship Hatti Buck *to Searsport, and ninety of us Searsport boys rode her back. We had never been south, except for a few that had fought in the war. We arrived in March of '74, when the weather was nice and the mosquitoes and alligators were still not out. Bucksville is about as far out in the country as you can get and there was nothing to do but work. Some of Henry Buck's freed slaves helped cut live oak for the frames. Jonathan Nichols and my boss, Elisha Dunbar, made the ship's model and laid out the full-scale plans. We built the launching site along the river and started laying the keel in June. By that time, the bugs, snakes and alligators were out, and some of the fellows were ready to go home. Henry Buck tried to make us comfortable, but where we were living was nothing but a camp. We ate stuff we had never tasted before, like grits and barbequed hog. In July, the temperature got up to around a hundred degrees, and it was so humid at night that it was almost impossible to sleep.*

At first, Elisha tried to keep us from drinking by not paying us, but we threatened to mutiny if he didn't let us get drunk on weekends. There were a couple of local boys making corn liquor, and we started buying it from them. That kept us quiet for a while, until July, when men began getting sick with malaria. About ten of them were sent home in August, almost dead. One man hanged himself. Elisha and William Buck were afraid we would all quit and steal his boat to go home, so he let us ride a steamboat into Georgetown, a few at a time, just for a change of scenery. At least there were some women around and plenty of booze. As you can imagine, some of us got into trouble, including me, and I ended up in jail for a couple of nights.

In spite of all those problems, we managed to get the hull built by October. The weather started to cool off, and the ones of us who were left began to get used to Bucksville and to think it wasn't so bad. The three masts were cut from the most beautiful southern longleaf pines that you ever saw. We couldn't step the masts because there were trees overhanging the river that were in the way. During the winter, we finished almost everything else. She was a beautiful ship.

It was May 1875 when we launched her. The launching was a gala event. There were five steamboats there, all loaded with people who came to watch. People came in every conceivable vehicle from at least fifty miles around. Jonathan Nichols's wife, who the ship was named for, christened the Henrietta. *The launching went perfectly. Elisha Dunbar knocked out the wedge, and she slid down the ways and into the Waccamaw River, easy as you please.*

Moby Dick had been taking swallows of rum between sentences, and his glass had been refilled.

A few days after the launching, a tug towed Henrietta *down the river to Georgetown, where there were no trees in the way. The masts were on deck, and we raised them with sheer-legs. That was when I had the most work to do. It took me and ten other men another month to finish rigging the shrouds, stays, halyards, sheets, booms, gaffs and everything else. Captain Nichols and the rest of the ship's officers came down from Searsport to get ready to sail her out of Georgetown and Winyah Bay. It was about that time that a Georgetown steamboat captain mentioned that the depth of Winyah Bay, in places, was less than eighteen feet on high tide. Even a spring tide wouldn't get the* Henrietta *over the bar.*

Moby Dick looked around the room to see that everybody in the bar was paying close attention.

Now, do you know who it was that came up with the idea of how to get her out of there? Can you guess who it was? It was me. I said to Elisha that there was only one way to do it. We made giant rafts out of big timbers. Then we strapped two hundred empty and sealed turpentine barrels to the underside of the rafts. Steamboats towed the Henrietta *down Winyah Bay on high tide until she went aground. Other steamboats towed the floating rafts to the same place. When the tide went out, the* Henrietta *careened onto her starboard side, and we floated the rafts of barrels under her and fastened the rafts together. When the five-foot tide came in, the* Henrietta *was floating higher. The steamboats towed her out until she was aground again. When the tide went out, we shifted the barrels lower. On the next high tide, the steamboats dragged the rafts supporting the* Henrietta *over the bar and into deep water. We flooded the barrels, a few at a time, and the* Henrietta *floated in twenty-six feet of water. She raised her sails, set out for St. John, New Brunswick, and never returned to Georgetown. Now, what do you think of that?*

One of the bar's patrons yelled out, "Well, if you're so smart, why are you here?"

He answered, "After we finished building her, launching her and leading her into deep water, almost everybody from Searsport went back home. A few stayed and married local southern girls. Most everybody had just come down here to build the *Henrietta* and were anxious to get back to their families. I was one who stayed."

"Why was that?" someone asked. Moby Dick took a final big swig of rum.

"That, gentlemen, is another story. I can only say that a beautiful woman, a scoundrel and a marlinspike were involved, and I was no longer welcome in Maine. Someday, I'll tell you the rest of that story." Moby Dick staggered to his feet, let out a loud fart and stumbled toward the door. Abram and his mate, George, helped Moby Dick into his bateau, and he began to row toward his derelict sailboat. As Abram and George walked back to the *Potter*, they talked about the beautiful square-riggers they had often admired, tied up along the South Street piers in New York City. They wondered if the *Henrietta* might have been one of the Down Easters they had seen during the *Potter*'s passages far out at sea, heading toward some foreign shore. Abram said he sometimes wished he had shipped out on one of those clipper ships.

Abram spent the Christmas holidays in Georgetown. Then the *Potter* was loaded with crossties and towed to the Atlantic, and her sails were raised and set. Out there, on the vast expanse of a cold sea, Abram knew he was where he belonged. He was an expert in his profession. He knew when to shorten sail, how to anticipate changes in the weather and what to say to motivate his men to do what needed to be done. He could do any job that any of his men could do, from repairing the donkey engine or a bilge pump to climbing the rigging to shift a topsail or splicing a cable. He could pull a man's tooth or sew up a wound when necessary. He was a strict disciplinarian who demanded the ship be kept in good order, but he rewarded good work with extra pay and time off. One or two of his crew members had left after one passage because they couldn't or wouldn't do the work, but most of his crew stayed on for a year or longer. His mate, George Pierson, was loyal and hardworking. The black cook served better-than-average grub and was able to prepare it in almost any kind of weather, and he stayed on voyage after voyage. By the time the *Potter* reached the sea buoy off New York, Abram was in a carefree spirit, looking forward to seeing his daughter and finding more cargo to take south.

He spent a week in Fairhaven with Lydia, Myra and Florence. Frederick had gone back to Brown, where he was at the top of his class and working on a thesis for his PhD. Florence was growing into a beautiful girl, and Lydia was educating her as fast as she could learn. Abram had sent a copy of his newspaper article to Lydia, who was impressed by his literary skills. She gave him a list of books that she thought he ought to read, including two new novels by Joseph Conrad.

Captain Slocum returned to New York and met with the agent for the *Potter*. The agent told Slocum that demand for southern hard pine was increasing more than ever throughout the Northeast. Business was booming, and the *Potter* had a backlog of orders. He also said that Georgetown was on its way to becoming one of the most important lumber ports on the East Coast. There were already three major sawmills in Georgetown, and a fourth—and much larger—one was considering moving there if the federal government finished construction of stone jetties at the Winyah Bay entrance, which would deepen the channel enough to accommodate steamships. He advised Slocum to consider switching over from sailing schooners to steamships because he thought that schooners would be obsolete within a few years. A steamship could haul twice as much lumber and make the passage in half the time that schooners took. Before Slocum left to go back to the *Potter*, the agent had signed him up for two solid years of hauling lumber from Gardner & Lacey Lumber Company in Georgetown to New York and Philadelphia.

Abram thought about his agent's advice about steamships. He never liked them—their noise, their dirty coal smoke and particularly their lack of romance. As long as he could stay busy on sailing schooners, he would stick to sailing. If he were to make a change, he would prefer to become captain of one of the clipper ships that sailed all over the world. Well, at least he knew what he would be doing for the next two years. *Georgetown's not so bad,* he thought.

The *Potter's* agent had also arranged for a steady series of southbound cargo passages, hauling salt or coal to Savannah. The round trips from Philadelphia or New York to Savannah, then to Georgetown and back north began in February 1895, averaging three months per round trip, some rough and some smooth. Each time the *Potter* approached the Georgetown entrance, the new granite jetties protruded a little farther out into the ocean, but they still had a long way to go. The draft of the *Potter* was shallow enough to be able to cross the bar on even the lowest tide. The *Potter* no longer loaded lumber up the Black River because Jacob Savage had bought property along the shore of the Sampit River and moved his sawmill operation away from Olivet. It was just too difficult and expensive for schooners to go that far up the Black River.

In October 1895, the *Potter* was heading south with a partial load of coal when Abram noted a sharp drop in the barometer and an increase in velocity of the east wind. He reduced sail and made ready to duck into Norfolk if necessary. He guessed there was a hurricane out there somewhere but had no way of gauging its strength or path. Within twelve hours, the wind had increased to fifty knots and remained strong through the rest of the night. By early morning, the wind had slowly dropped and shifted to the north and then to the northwest, so he knew the storm had veered out to sea. He put on more sail and changed the *Potter's* heading to southeast to clear Cape Hatteras. When he was thirty miles south of Hatteras, a lookout spotted a sailing vessel low in the water and under bare poles. The vessel showed distress signals, and Abram ordered the *Potter* to approach the vessel. Waves from the storm were still high. Through the glass, he made out the name *H.J. Cottrell* on the stern of a schooner, which was almost under water. Some men of her crew were waving white cloths. The *Potter* stood by for four hours until it was possible to launch the ship's yawl and row close enough to the *Cottrell* for her men to jump overboard and swim to the yawl. It took two trips by the yawl to rescue Captain Haskell and his crew of seven men. On October 14, the *Potter* was towed into Georgetown with the rescued men.

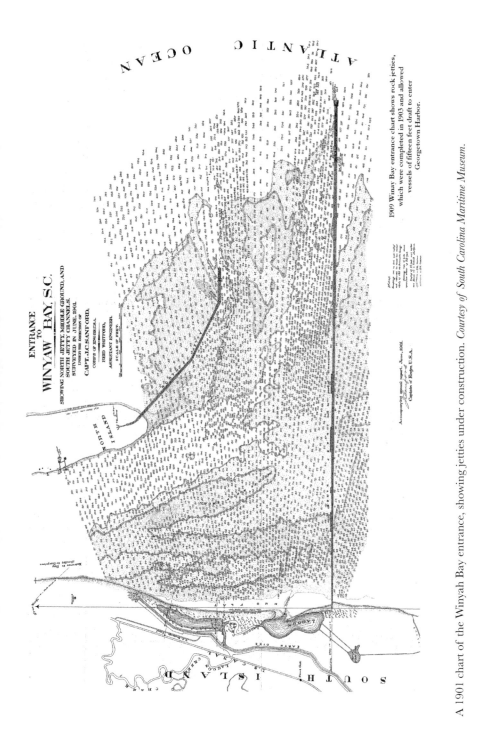

ENTRANCE
TO
WINYAW BAY, S.C.

SHOWING NORTH JETTY, MIDDLE GROUND, AND
SOUTH JETTY CHANNELS.
SURVEYED IN JUNE, 1901.
UNDER THE DIRECTION OF
CAPT. J.C. SANFORD,
CORPS OF ENGINEERS.
RICH WHITFORD,
ASSISTANT ENGINEER.
SCALE OF FEET

ATLANTIC OCEAN

NORTH ISLAND

SOUTH ISLAND

A 1901 chart of the Winyah Bay entrance, showing jetties under construction. *Courtesy of South Carolina Maritime Museum.*

1909 Winay Bay entrance chart shows rock jetties, which were completed in 1903 and allowed vessels of fifteen feet draft to enter Georgetown Harbor.

When sailors from other vessels in the port and the merchants of Front Street found out that Captain Slocum had rescued the crew of the schooner *H.J. Cottrell,* he was treated as a hero. At Maroneys Oyster Bar, Abram and his crew were given unlimited rounds of beer, and at intermission of the burlesque show at Steele's Opera House, Abram and his first mate were asked to stand and receive applause.

Throughout 1896, the *Potter* continued to make passages between Georgetown and Philadelphia, New York and Boston. In early May 1897, Abram was aboard the *Potter,* tied up in front of Gardner & Lacey, when two members of the Winyah Fire Company asked to speak with him. They said they would like to entertain some citizens of Georgetown with an excursion to North Island and wanted to know if Captain Slocum would allow his schooner to be used to transport the Winyah Fire Company and its guests to the Georgetown Lighthouse wharf on May 13. The tug *Congdon* had agreed to tow the schooner there and back. The *Potter* had just arrived from Savannah, and Captain Slocum told the firemen that the ship would need a thorough cleaning if she were to be used as an excursion boat. He said they could use her if the Winyah Fire Company helped with the cleaning. On May 13, the *Congdon* towed the *Potter* across the Sampit River to allow excursionists to board at the clock tower. On May 14, the *State* newspaper in Columbia, South Carolina, had this report:

> GEORGETOWN'S FIREMEN
> A DELIGHTFUL EXCURSION TO NORTH ISLAND GIVEN BY THEM
> *Special to* The State.
>
> *Georgetown, May 14.—Aboard the schooner* Warren B. Potter *the members of the Winyah Fire company yesterday gave their friends of Georgetown a most delightful excursion to North Island, distant about 12 miles from the city on the Sampit. This excursion is one of the annual social events of Georgetown and no one ever fails to attend. The second trip was scheduled to leave at 6 o'clock, but the people continued to arrive in such numbers that it was well after that hour before the tug* Congdon *started down the river and out into the open bay with the* Warren B. Potter *in tow.*
>
> *On the schooner all was life and merriment. The band played and the young folk danced to the music. Young America ran riot and played hide and seek from the very bottom of the schooner.*
>
> *On the way out refreshments of a substantial nature were served and the salt breeze only added to the zest in disposing of them. Soon after 9*

A dance hall at the base of the Georgetown Lighthouse Pier. *Courtesy of Georgetown County Digital Library, Tarbox Collection.*

o'clock North Island was reached. Here the young people broke up into twos and at convenient distances walked along the hard sandy beach. The moon shone bright and the night was such as lovers love. And judging from the interchange of tender looks, when the whistle of the Congdon *sounded the recall, there were not a few of them.*

The return was not less pleasant than the outgoing trip. Again dancing and refreshments kept all engaged until Georgetown was reached after 1 o'clock in the morning. The entire affair was most enjoyable.

During the excursion, Abram met Lillian Remine, secretary to the president of a new lumber company, the Atlantic Coast Lumber (ACL) Company, which was planning to build a large sawmill operation in Georgetown. Abram was much attracted to beautiful Lillian, who was the daughter of a fishing schooner captain in Salem, Massachusetts, and

Blair House on Front Street, across from the clock tower. *Courtesy of Georgetown County Digital Library.*

had just moved to Georgetown. He found out that she was rooming at the Blair House on Front Street, and he promised to visit her. He found his way to the boardinghouse on Monday afternoon. He and Lillian sat in a swing on the porch and found out more about each other. She was twenty-three and had never been married. Abram told her about his first marriage and about his daughter, Florence. They saw each other several times before the *Potter* was loaded with lumber and left for New York. Abram continued to court Lillian during subsequent voyages to Georgetown. They fell in love, and both of them knew they would spend the rest of their lives together.

In January 1898, Abram and the *Potter* were again in Georgetown. As they were securing to the Gardner & Lacey wharf, Abram noticed much commotion at the government pier, where workboats normally ferried materials unloaded from railroad cars to the jetty construction site. This time, there was a U.S. Navy launch, the *Water Lily*, tied up to the pier, and a procession of formally dressed men were climbing down from a private Pullman car and boarding the launch. The port pilot told Abram that the Pullman car was the "Davy Crockett" and that Ex-President Grover Cleveland was among those boarding the *Water Lily*. He was on his way to South Island to go duck hunting at the home of the famous Confederate General Alexander.

As soon as Abram left the *Potter*, he walked straight to Lillian's boardinghouse. She told Abram that she liked her job and her boss, Mr. Freeman S. Farr, president of Atlantic Coast Lumber Company, who had moved to Georgetown from the Midwest. She had learned that ACL had been founded by Wall Street tycoon Charles R. Flint, who had raised enough capital to secure options on many thousands of acres of timberland in coastal South Carolina. The company had incorporated in Norfolk, Virginia, where it was making plans for a huge sawmill to be located somewhere in Georgetown. At the moment, Farr, one attorney and Lillian were the only ones in Georgetown, and they were working out of a local attorney's office.

Before Abram left for another voyage to New York, he and Lillian decided to be married the next time he returned. Her father had died at sea, her mother was dead and she had no brothers or sisters, so Lillian had no desire for a fancy wedding. They decided to marry in the office of a justice of the peace in Georgetown. Abram wrote to Lydia and the rest of his family telling them of their decision. He knew his mother would be pleased that he was marrying a woman from Salem. He looked forward to the day when Lillian could meet them and his daughter would have a stepmother she could love.

It was May 1898 when Captain Slocum next brought the *Potter* into Winyah Bay. This time, the Winyah Bay entrance was teeming with activity. At the end of the jetties, huge brush mats, which had been built onshore and transported to the entrance to Winyah Bay, were being placed on the bottom. Large granite stones were piled on top of the mats. The stones were being unloaded by derricks from barges and schooners onto rail cars that transported them to the end of the north jetty, where they were lowered and piled up to form a barrier against the sea. So many barges, workboats and steam tugs were working at the entrance that it was difficult for the *Potter* to be towed past the activity and up the bay. Even the bay and the Sampit River were busy with more boats and ships than Abram had ever seen in Georgetown. Once they were tied up at Gardner & Lacey's wharf and Abram had seen that everything was in order, he hurried to Lillian's boardinghouse. She ran to him and gave him a long kiss.

Lillian had much to tell. When she had told Mr. Farr that she was going to be married, he and Mrs. Farr had insisted on being part of the wedding. Instead of a justice of the peace, they would be married in the law office where she worked. Mr. Farr's associate, an attorney, would perform the ceremony, and a reception would be held at the Farrs' home. Lillian said they were pleased with her work. She also said that everyone had heard about the famous Captain Slocum, who had saved the crews of two other schooners.

Lillian said that several more lawyers and engineers had been sent by the management of ACL to purchase more timberland and stumpage and to design and buy equipment for the sawmills. The company had purchased a site for the mill, located on the southernmost bend of the Sampit River. Part of the site had been Jacob Savage's sawmill, which had not been successful and had closed. The rest of the sawmill land had been Serenity Plantation, purchased by the mill from a group of Georgetown businessmen.

Abram had told the ship's agent that he was getting married in Georgetown and would delay the *Potter*'s sailing for a week in June. The agent was glad for the *Potter* to remain where she was, at least until the uncertainties of the Spanish-American War against Cuba were resolved. The crew was given a week off with pay. The wedding went as planned. Lillian was beautiful in a white gown she had purchased in Charleston. Abram had bought her ring in New York City. Freeman Farr acted in a very friendly manner toward Abram and was interested in hearing stories about his sea voyages. The reception at the Farrs' home was much bigger than Lillian had anticipated. Mrs. Farr had her large home elaborately decorated, and she invited many of the finest citizens of Georgetown, including Mayor Morgan, Heiman Kaminski, Louis Ehrich and many others. The big surprise was the appearance of Charles Flint, founder of the company. Lillian knew he was in Georgetown for a conference but hadn't expected him to attend her reception. He seemed most interested in meeting Captain Slocum. They stood together, talking about sailing. Flint told Abram that he was part owner of the latest America's Cup entry, the *Vigilant*. He was a sailing enthusiast and wanted his company to own a schooner to transport lumber. He knew that this was the Age of Steam, but he was still nostalgic for the Age of Sail. He knew that Abram commanded a three-masted schooner that had made many voyages into Georgetown. Flint wanted to build a new four-master. He told Abram to keep in touch with Freeman Farr about the possibility of commanding that schooner.

Lillian and Abram spent the first night of their married life aboard the *Potter*. They spent their honeymoon at a beach house on Pawleys Island owned by Atlantic Coast Lumber. At the end of the week, Lillian returned to her job at ACL and Abram returned to the *Potter*, which was already loaded with lumber.

In mid-July 1888, Abram received a letter from Lydia, enclosing a clipping from a July 10 Fairhaven newspaper:

> *An Intrepid Navigator: Capt. Slocum Arrives in Fairhaven from a Voyage Around the World.*
>
> *The captain came to Fairhaven for a little rest, to put the* Spray *back in condition, and renew his acquaintance with his many friends in Fairhaven. The hold of the* Spray *is filled with all kinds of curiosities gathered from various parts of the world. Judging from the books of newspaper clippings in the captain's possession, he is considered an excellent lecturer and has been honored by high officials everywhere. He has a stereopticon and 300 excellent slides, which he uses to illustrate his lectures.*
>
> *Captain Slocum says he intends to remain around here a few days and will then go cruising with his wife and son. He intends to go to London before long.*

Lydia said in her letter that this Captain Joshua Slocum might be a distant cousin, although he had grown up in Nova Scotia. She had never heard of him before he arrived in Fairhaven. He apparently was the first man to circumnavigate the globe in a small sailboat, single-handed. She and Florence had walked down to the waterfront to see his vessel, which was very small to have crossed all those oceans. She wished that Abram were there to see the *Spray* and meet his distant cousin. Abram had heard of Joshua Slocum but had never met him.

In late September 1898, Abram and the *Potter* provisioned and made ready to deliver a load of lumber from Georgetown to Boston. In addition to the normal foodstuffs taken aboard for the voyage, the cook had bought a gallon of shucked raw oysters at the last minute from a fisherman who rowed up alongside in his flat-bottomed bateau. After the *Potter* had crossed the bar, let the pilot off and set sail, the cook served all members of the crew a big bowl of oyster stew for dinner. By midnight, every man on the schooner, including Abram, was deathly sick. They vomited and suffered from diarrhea, cramps and extreme stomach pain.

No one was fit for duty at the wheel or even as lookout. As morning approached, the *Potter* was near the latitude of Frying Pan Shoals, a few miles off the entrance to the Cape Fear River. Abram managed to crawl to the wheel and steer south of Frying Pan Shoals Lightship toward Southport. The engineer was unable to man the donkey engine, so George Pierson and one other man dropped the sails and let go the anchors in thirty feet of water just off Southport. When the pilot came alongside, Abram was able to put a ladder over the side and explain that they needed a doctor. An hour later, a doctor from Southport came on board, diagnosed the problem as food poisoning and suggested that a tug tow them into Southport Harbor so they could stay ashore until they were well enough to sail. Within two days, the crew had recovered. After they had cursed the cook for buying raw oysters in a hot-weather month, they got underway and made an uneventful passage to Boston.

The following year, in June 1899, Lillian was given a vacation from her job to join Abram on a passage from Georgetown to New York. It was Lillian's first deep-sea, long-distance passage. She was not seasick and was as enthralled by the sea as Abram had been on his first voyage. They had a smooth passage of eight days. The *Potter* was becalmed off Cape Fear for part of one day, rolling slightly in the long swells. Abram had the yawl boat launched and dragged behind the *Potter* while he and Lillian dove into the warm water of the Gulf Stream, where they held onto a line behind the yawl. Later, they fished and caught several dolphins. Lillian joined the cook in the galley and helped to prepare a delicious fish dinner for the crew.

One night, they stood watch together on the quarterdeck. Whitecaps dotted the surface of the black water. Phosphorescent particles of green light streamed out behind the rudder. Every few seconds, the stern of the schooner was lifted slightly by an ocean swell. The only sounds were the swoosh of water running past the hull and the creaking of ropes when the wind strained against the sails. Looking up, they watched the tops of the masts and sails cut across millions of stars fixed in a moonless sky. Except for a faint light from the ship's compass, there was darkness all around them. Abram was glad that Lillian could share the peace that he always felt in sailing his ship through the night.

Lillian had never visited New York City. Abram sailed the *Potter* up the Sandy Hook Channel and anchored, as he normally did. A pilot came aboard, and a tug was secured alongside. The weather was warm and clear at midday as the tug approached the city. Lillian began to see tall buildings in the distance. When the tug passed between Staten Island and Brooklyn and made a starboard turn toward Manhattan, Lillian was looking directly at the Statue of Liberty and the skyline of New York City. She was astonished by the immensity of so many big buildings in front of her and so much boat and ship traffic all around her. When they passed between the Statue of Liberty and Governors Island, Ellis Island was to port. The immigration building had burned in 1897 and was being rebuilt. Lillian looked up in awe at the graceful span of the Brooklyn Bridge as they passed under it. She couldn't believe the number of vessels of all types plying back and forth and the number of huge steamships tied up along both sides of the East River. There were also beautiful sailing ships. Some were three- and four-masted schooners, and others were square-rigged ships. The excitement was over too soon as they approached an industrial lumber pier in Brooklyn where the *Potter* would unload her cargo. When the *Potter* was tied up and squared away at the Brooklyn wharf, Abram and Lillian left the ship in charge of the mate. There wasn't much time for Lillian to sightsee in New York City, but they were able to take a quick tour of part of the city on a tram before heading for the train station.

That evening, they took the train to New Bedford so that Lillian could meet Abram's family. Lillian and Florence, then twelve years old, bonded immediately. Florence had become a beautiful girl. Lillian got along well with Lydia and Myra. Frederick Jr. brought his fiancée, Carrie, to Fairhaven to meet Lillian. Frederick taught astronomy at Brown University. He and Carrie were to be married in New Bedford later that same month. After two days, Abram took Lillian to the station in New Bedford to catch a train south. It was now possible to go all the way to Georgetown by train, and Lillian had to return to work.

By the end of 1899, Atlantic Coast Lumber Company's sawmills, kilns, shops, foundry, power plant, offices, store, hotel and many employees' houses were well underway and nearing completion. It was a huge complex with almost 1,500 people employed in the construction and operation of the facility. They were building a shipping warehouse and loading wharf projecting 1,200 feet out into the Sampit River. The wharf was capable of storing two and a half million feet of lumber and loading three ships at a time. The company had extended and improved the railroads into Georgetown and Horry Counties so that more logs could be brought into the mill. All facilities within the mill were connected by electrically operated trams. The equipment was driven by steam and electricity produced in its

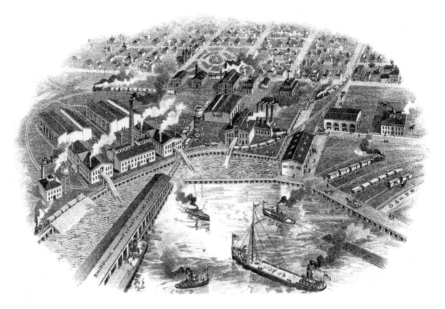

1902 Atlantic Coast Lumber Company letterhead. *Courtesy of South Carolina Maritime Museum.*

own power plant. According to management, this mill was going to be the most modern and largest one in the world.

Three other major sawmills and several smaller mills were already producing millions of board feet of lumber, beams, crossties, poles, shingles and barrels, both pine and cypress, all being cut from the forests of coastal Carolina. In addition, there were still farmers along the rivers who were tapping what was left of the longleaf pine trees for turpentine, rosin and pitch. All these products were being shipped by steamship and schooner to the northeastern United States. While Abram was being towed up Winyah Bay, he watched almost twenty other schooners arriving, departing or being loaded, not to mention four or five big steamships, dozens of tugboats, river steamers, lighters, barges and workboats. The 160-foot stack of the ACL power plant was visible from far out at sea, and the jetties were extending thousands of feet into the ocean from North Island and South Island. Abram felt he was part of the industrial revolution of South Carolina, all based on an adequate supply of big trees. He wondered how long the supply would last.

Lillian still lived at the boardinghouse while Abram was away and aboard the *Potter* when Abram was in Georgetown. She dreaded his leaving for each voyage and longed for his return. In July 1900, she told Abram that she was pregnant. She and Abram knew that she couldn't continue to work and live in a boardinghouse. She would need to be with family and friends, which meant quitting her job and moving somewhere close to Fairhaven. Lillian had enjoyed her friends and associates at ACL but had never felt completely at home in the South. She looked forward to living among people she had grown up with and taking care of her stepdaughter. Abram and Lillian planned for Lillian to move into Lydia's house in Fairhaven in November.

In late September, the *Potter* was being loaded for a voyage to Philadelphia, and Abram knew that he probably wouldn't see Lillian again before she moved away from Georgetown. On a Sunday afternoon, they were walking along Front Street toward Lillian's boardinghouse when Eddie Kaminski caught up with them and gave them a warning. He told them that the day before, a black barber, John Brownfield, had shot and killed a deputy sheriff. It had happened only a few blocks from where they were heading. Brownfield had been arrested and was in jail. There was a rumor that a gang of the deputy's white friends was planning to storm the jail, take Brownfield away and lynch him. Eddie warned them to stay away from that part of town. Heeding his warning, Abram and Lillian returned to the *Potter*. The next day, Abram was told by one of his crew that there had been a confrontation on Sunday evening between whites and one thousand blacks, who gathered at the jail to defend Brownfield. The black women were particularly protective, wielding pitchforks and hoes. A shot had been fired, which had wounded Doar, the newspaper editor. Only the calm intervention of Mayor Morgan had prevented a race riot. The situation was still not settled.

On Monday afternoon, Abram and Lillian watched as a large troop of uniformed white soldiers arrived from Sumter and Charleston and gathered along Front Street. They formed a long line, four abreast, and paraded through the city, carrying rifles and pulling a Gatling gun on a carriage. They made a real show of force, which had the effect they wanted to make on the black population. There was no race riot, and the situation quieted down. On Tuesday, Abram made sure the city was safe before walking Lillian back to the boardinghouse. He kissed her goodbye, returned to the *Potter* and got underway for Philadelphia.

Once they were out at sea, Abram heard the details of the murder from his mate. According to all that the mate had heard, a deputy had entered Brownfield's barbershop on Saturday afternoon with a warrant for

Brownfield to pay his overdue poll tax bill. Brownfield had refused to pay. When Brownfield dropped the straight razor that he was using to shave a customer, the deputy bent down to pick it up for him. When he did, his revolver fell out of his holster. Brownfield grabbed the pistol and shot the deputy five times. Brownfield ran out the back door but was caught by a policeman. He was to be tried soon and would probably be hanged for murder, as he should be, according to the mate.

Abram's black cook listened as the mate told what happened. The cook waited until the mate left the cabin before saying to Abram:

> *That ain't what happened, Captain. I was there. I was in the barbershop on Saturday afternoon when this white man shoves his way in and tells John Brownfield to pay his poll tax now, if he knew what was good for him. John had a customer in the chair, and he told this man that he couldn't pay it right then. That made the white man angry, and he goes right up to John, pulls out a big pistol, puts it right up to John's head and tells him to pay or he would kill him. Well, John dropped the razor he was using and grabbed at the pistol before the man could shoot him. They wrestled with that gun, and it went off and hit the white man in the stomach. That didn't stop the white man from trying to get the gun back, but it went off again and again. The man ran out the door, holding his stomach, and fell down in the street, yelling for help. John didn't know what to do, and he ran out the back door and climbed a fence. I saw the whole thing, Captain.*

"Why didn't you tell the police that story?"

"Ha! I know what them white policemen would say. They wouldn't believe me, and even if they did, they would shut me up. I know better than to argue with them. I came on back to the ship, and I ain't going to say nothing." Nothing more was said about the incident.

In November 1900, Lillian said goodbye to her friends and caught the train to New Bedford. She moved temporarily into Lydia's house in Fairhaven. Her daughter, Marjorie, was born in February 1901, while Abram was at sea.

Lillian had helped Abram keep in contact with Freeman Farr and other officials of the ACL regarding the possible building of a schooner. Meanwhile, in 1900, ACL had leased and put into service two new steel steamships, the *Waccamaw* and the *Georgetown*, each of which could transport over 1,250,000 feet of lumber. They were 250 feet long, 40 feet wide and drew 18 feet of water, so they were dependent on the greater depth of Winyah Bay after the jetties were constructed and the channel dredged to a depth of 15 to 18 feet. The jetties were completed in 1902.

At the end of 1901, Freeman Farr contacted Abram Slocum and told him that Charles Flint had decided that ACL would lease a new four-masted schooner, to be built in Bath, Maine, in 1902 and named the *City of Georgetown*. When Abram met Farr in his office, Farr asked how Lillian was getting along. He spoke about how fond he and his associates had become of Lillian, how they missed her vivacious enthusiasm and how he had hoped that Abram and she would have made their home in Georgetown. He then asked Abram if he would agree to oversee the construction of the schooner and be her captain. Abram readily agreed.

Chapter 5

MASTER OF THE FOUR-MASTED
SCHOONER *CITY OF GEORGETOWN*

(1902–1907)

Abram contacted the *Potter*'s agent in New York and submitted his resignation. His agent expressed sorrow at Abram's leaving but understood his desire to command a larger vessel. He told Abram that Captain Hammett would be relieving him. Abram's first mate, George Pierson, said he would stay with the *Potter* until the *City of Georgetown* was launched, at which point he would join Abram. Abram made his last voyage on the *Warren B. Potter* in December 1901, leaving the vessel with Captain Hammett in Brooklyn.

Abram spent the rest of the winter with Lillian, Marjorie, Florence and the rest of his family. He bought a small house in Somerville, Massachusetts, near where Lillian had grown up and had friends, and moved there with his family. In February 1902, Abram Slocum caught the train to Bath, Maine, and reported to the Rogers Shipyard, where the *City of Georgetown*'s keel would be laid in March. Abram met William Rogers, the dean of Bath shipbuilders. They got along well together even though Rogers told Abram that he had warned his fellow shipbuilders twenty years earlier that it was inevitable that wooden ships would give way to iron vessels and that Bath must build iron vessels or none at all. That was why, he told Abram, the *City of Georgetown* would be the last wooden sailing vessel that his yard would build. Mr. Rogers said in a newspaper announcement that the *City of Georgetown* was the 100th vessel to be constructed in his shipyard and that she "would be the handsomest craft of her size to engage in the lumber business." Abram found a room in Bath where he could spend his nights, but he was up early and arrived at Rogers Shipyard every morning

The schooner *City of Georgetown* under construction in Bath, Maine, 1902. *Courtesy of Maine Maritime Museum.*

City of Georgetown oak deck beams weigh almost a ton each. *Courtesy of Maine Maritime Museum.*

City of Georgetown is planked with southern yellow hard pine. *Courtesy of Maine Maritime Museum.*

before eight o'clock. He watched Mr. Rogers and his master builder, H.E. Worsham, create the scale half model, molding the wood until the hull looked just the right shape. Then, they translated the shape of the hull, full-size, onto the lofting floor. From the full-sized measurements, the keel, stem and other elements of the vessel were sawn and shaped from white oak timbers. The keel was laid and fastened together on blocking at the slip where the vessel would be launched. After the keel was laid, each heavy oak frame was fabricated on a flat surface and raised into place by blocks and tackle on ginpoles pulled by mules. The frames were fastened into place, forming the skeleton of the vessel.

Lillian wrote to Abram each week, saying how much she missed him and how much she and the girls wished they could make a journey to Bath to see him and the new ship. Abram arranged for her, Florence and Marjorie, who was almost two years old, to come and stay with him for a week during the summer. While they were there, Abram gave them a tour of the partially built

Above: The only known photo of A.J. Slocum and his daughter Florence, in the wheelhouse of the *City of Georgetown*. *Courtesy of Maine Maritime Museum.*

Opposite top: Lillian and Marjorie Slocum seated on the frames of the *City of Georgetown*, 1902. *Courtesy of Maine Maritime Museum.*

Opposite bottom: Deck construction for the *City of Georgetown*, summer 1902. *Courtesy of Maine Maritime Museum.*

schooner and photographed them as they posed inside the ship's structure and seated on timbers that would become the masts of the *City of Georgetown*. They returned to Somerville at the end of the week.

After all the frames were in place and the bow and stern framing had been completed, a massive oak keelson was built up over the keel and frames, strengthening the ship from one end to the other. The keel, frame and keelson were fastened together with galvanized iron spikes and bolts and with hundreds of sledge-driven treenails. Next, the ceilings, rows of heavy interior planks of southern pine, some of which might have been delivered to Bath from forests near Georgetown, were run from bow to stern and fastened to the inside of the frames. Fourteen- by sixteen-inch oak deck beams, some over thirty-five feet long and weighing almost a ton, were hoisted into place. Planks of southern pine were bent along the outside of the frames, fastened, caulked with cotton and oakum and

Masts of the *City of Georgetown* have been stepped. *Courtesy of Maine Maritime Museum.*

Launching of the *City of Georgetown* in the Kennebec River, November 1902. *Courtesy of Maine Maritime Museum.*

sealed with pitch. The bowsprit, jib boom and rudder were constructed. Deck planking was laid, the forward and aft houses were constructed, the three deck hatches were built and the solid rail was constructed. She was one of the first schooners to have an enclosed wheelhouse to protect the steersman and the binnacle from the weather. A lifting frame, called sheer legs, was set on deck to steady the lifting of each eighty-foot-tall mast by the donkey engine. The four masts were of Oregon pine, delivered by rail from the West Coast. Thick strands of iron cables formed the standing rigging, holding the masts in place.

It took more than thirty skilled shipwrights and laborers, working long hours for four months, to complete the framing and planking, making the ship watertight. Joinerwork, trim, rigging, piping, machinery and painting were all completed by the end of October 1902. Two three-thousand-pound anchors were hoisted aboard. Booms, gaffs, topsail masts, running rigging and sails were all completed before the *City of Georgetown* was ready for launching on November 1. The entire construction process had taken only six months.

The launching of a four-masted schooner at any of the shipyards of Bath was a big event. Most of the citizens turned out to see the 180-foot schooner slide down the ways and into the Kennebec River, where more wooden sailing ships were launched than anywhere else in the country. Abram's whole family was there. Beautiful Florence christened the ship, swinging a bottle of champagne across the bow of the *City of Georgetown*. Abram bragged to Lydia and Lillian that his cabin was one of the largest and had the finest finishes of any four-masted schooner in the fleet. He showed them one bulkhead of his cabin that was covered in bookshelves fitted with fiddles to keep books from falling out. Abram was as proud of the launching of his new ship as anything that had ever happened in his life. The same could be said for Lydia, whose eldest son was her pride and joy. She wished that her husband, Frederick, could have seen this event.

The William Rogers & Son shipbuilding firm had started operation in 1847. The elder Rogers died in 1864, but William Rogers Jr. continued until 1902, when the last schooner, the *City of Georgetown*, was launched. The Bath newspaper reported:

Because this was the one hundredth ship launched at the William Rogers Shipyard, great admiration was shown for it. William Rogers claimed that the quality and speed in building this vessel was the best record ever made by an individual builder. A banquet, as well as the usual launching ceremonies marked the event, and the master builder, H.E. Worsham, was presented with a gold watch, chain and K. of P. charm by the men who worked under him and others interested as a testimonial to his excellent service and courteous way of executing his task. During the launching, the City of Georgetown *floated colors that day, presented by Mayor Morgan of Georgetown, and her cabin contained a number of souvenirs by friends. Among them was a set of doileys worked by the children of the North Bath Grammar School.*

The schooner *City of Georgetown* was registered in New Bedford, whose name was lettered in gold across her stern. Her permanent Enrollment Document of November 1902 listed fifty owners of the vessel, including twenty-three from New Bedford and nine from Georgetown. Those from Georgetown were George Easton, Fannie W. Hazzard, Ida G. Watts, Irene G. Potter, Alexander B. Potter, Charles L. Ford, James F. Doran, Benjamin D. Bourne and John M. Johnson. Abram J. Slocum owned a ³⁄₆₄ share. The largest shareholder was George W. Dibble, who owned a ⁴⁄₆₄ share.

As of the day after the launching, Captain Slocum assumed complete responsibility for the vessel as she lay alongside a wharf at Rogers Shipyard. His first mate, along with the rest of the crew, arrived in Bath, moved aboard and began carrying out duties necessary to provision the vessel and make her ready to get underway. The schooner carried a twenty-one-foot, gasoline-powered yawl boat hung from davits at the stern and a seventeen-foot rowing boat on deck. On November 28, the *City of Georgetown* was towed out of the Kennebec River, her sails were raised and she was underway on her maiden voyage to Georgetown, South Carolina. She proved to be a fast and easily handled ship, and she arrived at the Georgetown bar on December 3. Abram noticed that both of the impressive rock jetties were complete. The *City of Georgetown* was towed up the bay by the *Congdon* and secured to a wharf in front of the town clock tower.

The next day was open house on the *City of Georgetown*. Abram had worked his crew overtime to make the schooner perfect in every detail. Sail covers were stretched tight, lines coiled neatly and flags dressed the ship. All day long, dignitaries and crowds of city citizens visited the ship. The *Georgetown Times* reported:

After the maiden voyage of the *City of Georgetown* to Georgetown, South Carolina, citizens tour the schooner in December 1902. *Courtesy of Georgetown County Digital Library.*

Captain A.J. Slocum greets guests at the aft cabin of the *City of Georgetown. Courtesy of Georgetown County Digital Library.*

She received a big ovation from our city. The whistles blew and the bell rang, announcing her arrival. The dimensions of the vessel are as follows: Length, 168.7 feet; breadth, 36.4 feet; depth, 12.6 feet; and her gross tonnage is 599. The new vessel is equipped with all the latest improvements in the way of rigging, steam pumps and winches, cabin and galley furnishings and arrangements.

The City of Georgetown *is a beauty. Her lines are perfect. She has a single deck and a short poop deck. The captain's quarters and that for the first officer are finished in white wood and cherry. The captain's room is large and commodious and is situated on the starboard side and at the after end of the cabin. In the room is a desk of quartered oak and there are several large closets and numerous chart racks. The furniture is the best, and Capt. Slocum enjoys the comforts of home life while on the deep blue sea.*

Opening off the after companionway, which leads from the wheelhouse, is the bathroom. This has a fine tub and the improved marine lavatory arrangements. The after cabin occupies the main part of the house forward of the captain's apartments and bathroom. It is furnished with comfortable quartered oak furniture handsomely upholstered in green and is a well-lighted, cozy apartment.

The dining room is just forward of the after cabin and is also home-like and comfortably furnished, well-lighted and ventilated.

The forecastle, galley and engine room occupy the forward house. The City of Georgetown *has accommodation for four seamen besides her master, two mates, cook and engineer.*

The schooner spreads 4,500 yards of canvas and the sails are machine sewed and of first quality.

Abram was glad when the open house was over. A chain was put across the gangway, and a crewman was stationed on deck for security. Abram gave the rest of the crew liberty. He retired into his cabin, straightened things up and poured himself a drink. He had declined invitations by friends to eat and drink with them. There would be a banquet at the Palmetto Club the next night in his and the new schooner's honor. He thought about his new fame. He had never had so many strangers shake his hand, pat him on the back and tell him what a hero he was. *It won't last long,* he thought. He thought back to the time when Lillian had introduced him to Farr and Flint. If it hadn't been for Lillian, none of this would have ever happened. He wished she were here to share it with

Georgetown's Front Street during the 1905 centennial celebration. *Courtesy of Georgetown County Digital Library.*

him. She seemed happy, though, in their new house with Marjorie and Florence. He would tell them about it when he saw them next. For now, he would just enjoy himself.

The next morning, a Friday, Abram walked down Front Street for the first time in almost a year. Things had changed. New stores had been built, and more were under construction. There were concrete sidewalks alongside the street. Telephone and telegraph wires were strung on poles. Trees had been planted. There was a new drugstore and a bank. There were many more people on the streets, horses and carriages, more activity. People seemed in a hurry. As he walked, strangers greeted him, smiled and rushed by. He stopped in at Kaminski Hardware and talked with Joe Kaminski, who was running the store. Joe told Abram that they were the busiest they had ever been. He told him that Abram's old ship, the *Potter*, had just finished loading lumber at Winyah Lumber Company a few days ago. He said the *Golden Ball*, whose captain was a friend of Abram's, was in Georgetown. Abram continued walking, stopping at the C.L. Ford Ship Chandlery. The clerks told Abram that things were booming. He walked down Wood Street to the Clyde Steamship terminal. A ship was in. He climbed the stair and asked if Eddie Kaminski was in. Eddie came out with a big smile and shook Abram's hand.

"We've missed you. How's Lillian? Big night tonight. We'll see you at the Palmetto Club bar at six o'clock. I've got to go." Eddie was a few years younger than Abram. He had escorted Lillian a few times before she became engaged to Abram. Abram continued his walk. Ahead, he watched a trainload of logs crossing Front Street on the way into the Atlantic Coast Lumber Company's sawmills. He turned around before he reached the ACL complex of huge buildings and smokestacks. Before he went back to his ship, he stopped in at Crowleys Grocery and Ice House and ordered five hundred pounds of ice to be delivered Monday.

That evening, he and First Mate George Pierson walked to the Palmetto Club, where they were greeted by members and led into the crowded bar, buzzing with conversation and veiled in cigar smoke. Abram knew many of the members and was introduced to others. Among those whom he hadn't met previously were several of the nine Georgetown owners of the *City of Georgetown*. They were all looking forward to receiving handsome profits from the vessel's voyages. Also there were executives of Atlantic Coast Lumber Company, most of the merchants of the city and Mayor Morgan. Freeman Farr was there and asked about Lillian. After cocktail hour, everyone took their seats in the dining room. Abram and George Pierson were seated at the head table, along with Mayor Morgan, Heiman Kaminski, Eddie Kaminski and C.L. Ford. They ate a sumptuous meal, and then toasts were offered to the future of Georgetown, to the glorious dead of the Confederacy, to the *City of Georgetown* and her officers and to the glory of southern womanhood. Mayor Morgan made a twenty-minute speech, ending with praise for the gallant captain of Georgetown's new and beautiful schooner, followed by extended applause. Captain Slocum thanked the members of the Palmetto Club and their guests and expressed hope for continuing prosperity for all. Everyone adjourned to the bar. Abram and Eddie Kaminski had a couple of brandies together. Abram happened to remember the barber-murder incident and asked Eddie what happened. Eddie said that he had been a member of the jury that convicted John Brownfield and sentenced him to be hanged. Brownfield's lawyer had appealed and asked that the sentence be reduced, but the appeal failed. Eddie said that Brownfield would be hanged soon. Abram told Eddie that he had heard that Brownfield acted in self-defense. Eddie said no, there was no doubt in the jury's mind that Brownfield had committed murder and deserved to die. He asked Abram if he would like to go duck hunting the next morning. Abram declined because

The schooners *City of Georgetown* and *Charles Wittmore* load lumber at Atlantic Coast Lumber Company Pier. *Courtesy of Georgetown County Digital Library.*

he had to get the schooner ready to move over to the Atlantic Coast Lumber pier on Monday.

On Monday, the *City of Georgetown* was towed across the Sampit River to the long loading pier at Atlantic Coast Lumber Company. There were already two steamships tied up there, and the *City of Georgetown* was squeezed between them. Abram hated to see his pristine vessel ruined by scratching the newly finished decks and rails with piles of lumber. The stevedore foreman told Abram it would be at least another day before they would start loading his ship. They were behind with the loading of the two steamships, each of which carried twice what the *City of Georgetown* would hold. Abram stood and watched black stevedores hoist heavy boards on their shoulders and struggle to bring them to a cargo hatch, where others stacked them in the hold. There must have been fifty men working each ship, but it was a slow process. Sweat ran down their backs, even though it was a cold day. Occasionally, a foreman yelled for someone to speed up or stop loafing.

The captain of the steamship *Waccamaw* walked over to the *City of Georgetown* and asked Abram if he could come aboard. They shook hands, and he complimented Abram on the beauty and squared-away look of his schooner. He said he used to command schooners, but he had switched over to steam when he saw the handwriting on the wall. In some ways, he said, he wished he were back on sailing ships—the freedom, the quiet, the small crews, the feeling that you had your own little kingdom. He had a crew of thirty-five men on the *Waccamaw* shoveling coal and tending the engines, boilers and other equipment. There was always something going wrong. He guessed his pay was better, so it was worth it. He said he didn't like Georgetown or any place in the South, for that matter. He was from New Jersey and wished he were back there. If they would ever finish loading his ship, he stood a chance of being home for Christmas, he said. If the weather was decent, he could make New York in three days. He complained about the black stevedores. They were slow and lazy. But then, what could you expect from men who made seventy cents a day. He had heard a rumor that they were going to fire all the blacks and replace them with Italians, imported just to work the Georgetown docks. He guessed it would never happen because they would have to pay them too much. He and Abram gammed on until the *Waccamaw*'s captain was called back to his ship.

On Tuesday, loading of the *City of Georgetown* had still not started. Abram had listened to the roar of the sawmills and the whistles of steam locomotives hauling in logs for most of the morning. He watched steam tugboats tow long rafts of logs up the Sampit River, depositing them along the edge of a vast floating field of logs. He could see a conveyor pulling logs out of the floating field and up a ramp to one of the three sawmills. Electrically powered trams on tracks silently moved carloads of lumber from place to place. Abram asked a stevedore foreman if he could take a tour of the mill.

A few minutes later, an office clerk appeared and offered to show Abram around. They climbed stairs to the second level of one of the sawmills. The three sawmills together could process 2,500 logs per day. A steam-powered hoist lifted logs up from below and positioned them in front of multiple blades of giant belt-driven band saws. Logs were fed lengthwise by a conveyor into the teeth of the saw blades, which sliced the logs into wide boards. Other saws trimmed stacks of boards to correct widths and fed them down a ramp onto tram cars. The waste slabs were fed onto other trams, which transported the slabs and sawdust to furnaces to become fuel to heat steam that turned turbines and made electricity for the whole mill. The clerk showed Abram where lumber trams stopped in front of a double row of eighteen kiln buildings. Stacks of boards filled each of the kilns and were dried by steam pipes. The dried boards were either sent to a planing mill or stacked in storage piles until they were transported to the wharf building to be loaded onto the ships.

They walked through other buildings—a machine shop with many large lathes, presses and drills all driven by overhead belts; a foundry with multiple furnaces and stacks of iron plates and bars; a power plant with its furnaces, boilers, steam engines and electrical generators; and a turpentine plant and distillery where resin from the kilns and furnaces was distilled into the valuable byproduct. All this equipment was operated by skilled men, many recruited from cities in the North, and laborers from Georgetown and surrounding rural farms. Local black and white men also furnished labor to run the trams and trains to build the tracks and cut the trees and load logs onto trains or into the rivers for transit to the mill. All told, there were almost two thousand men working for Atlantic Coast Lumber Company to turn pine trees into lumber, not counting the crews of twenty or thirty steamships and schooners, which transported the lumber from Georgetown to the North.

Abram was shown the main office building, where fifty clerks, accountants, stenographers, attorneys, agents and managers shuffled papers to keep the mill processes going. When Lillian had worked for ACL, this building didn't exist. They walked over to the company store, which was in competition with Georgetown's stores to sell clothing, dry goods, groceries and appliances to the company's employees. Employees were paid in part with tokens, which could be redeemed only at the company store. Georgetown's merchants grumbled about that arrangement, but there was nothing they could do about it. Next to the company store was a company hotel, where traveling executives and newly hired employees could stay until housing was available. The store, office and hotel fronted on Fraser Street, which was the main route south toward Charleston and north to Front Street. The clerk pointed out that the company was building houses for its new employees as quickly as possible because there were no other houses available in Georgetown. The houses, a park and a church were across Fraser Street on property owned by ACL.

Abram walked back to his ship. He was amazed by this big-city Yankee operation, transported to the rural South. It was being run by New York businessmen, and he was sure they were getting most of the benefit from it. He realized that he was only a little cog in a big machine. They had leased his ship, and he would have to do what they told him to do. In a way, he wished he were back on the *Warren B. Potter*, which was a much more informal and relaxed arrangement, where he had more freedom to do what he wanted. *Oh well,* he thought, *when I'm out on the ocean, I'm as free as ever. I have a beautiful new schooner, well built and fast, and it's a pleasure to sail it.*

Two more days passed before the steamships were loaded and had steamed away. The two of them carried a total of almost 3 million feet of lumber and might be unloading in New York in four days. The *City of Georgetown* would carry 600,000 feet of lumber and could take two weeks to reach New York, depending on the wind. It was almost January, and northeast winds wouldn't help Abram sail where he wanted to go. A northeasterly gale delayed departure until the first week of January 1903. The *City of Georgetown* reached New York City ten days later. The ship was towed to a new and modern wharf facility owned by ACL, where cranes and stevedores unloaded the cargo in less than three days. Abram had anticipated going home for a few days before picking up another cargo and heading south, but the efficient ACL agent had already arranged for the *City of Georgetown* to load other cargo and return south.

It was another two months before Abram was in port long enough to return to Somerville for a week to see his family. All was well. He helped celebrate Florence's birthday. Lydia took a train from Fairhaven, and Frederick came up from Brown University. Abram played with his little daughter, went fishing with his brother and reunited with Lillian, who he hadn't seen in four months. Lillian could see that her husband was proud of his new schooner and was enjoying his life, but she wished he could be with his family more often. He returned to his ship and made another passage to Georgetown. Some necessary repair of the donkey engine kept the *City of Georgetown* in port for two weeks, awaiting parts from Maine, so Abram had a chance for a vacation.

He contacted his friend Eddie Kaminski, who suggested that they spend a couple of days surf fishing on Pawleys Island, where his family owned a beach house. Abram said he wanted to ride on the steamboat that the Atlantic Coast Lumber Company had bought to ferry employees back and forth to the beach. They had not only bought the steamboat *Governor Safford* to take passengers from Georgetown to Hagley Landing on the Waccamaw River behind Pawleys Island but had also built a five-mile railroad track from Hagley Landing to Pawleys Island. Abram and

The *Governor Safford* lands passengers at Hagley Landing to catch the train to Pawleys Island. *Courtesy of Georgetown County Digital Library.*

A sketch of Kaminski "Summer Academy," Pawleys Island, South Carolina. *Courtesy of Mary McAlister.*

Eddie boarded the side-wheeler, along with a few other local citizens. The captain blew his whistle, and they were underway on a twelve-mile trip up the Waccamaw River.

They reached Hagley Landing in a little over an hour, disembarked and boarded an old passenger car that was coupled to an even older steam locomotive. There was no place for the engine to turn around, so the train went forward to the island and backed up from Pawleys Island to Hagley Landing. The train was a real tourist attraction, and Georgetown families loved to entertain their children with all-day excursions to Pawleys Island and back. ACL had also built a large beach hotel south of the train's termination point where executives and important visitors could stay.

Eddie and Abram caught a ride on a wagon to the Kaminski property, which was almost the southernmost house on the island. The house was about fifty yards back from the beach, separated by sand dunes over twenty feet high. Eddie said that the old house had been built before the Civil War and had acted as a summer academy for children of wealthy rice planters who spent their summers on Pawleys Island. The rice planters and their families would leave their plantations along the Waccamaw River when the weather was hot enough for miasma and mosquitoes to breed in the rice fields and swamps close to the river. They would leave overseers and slaves behind to tend their plantations.

Eddie unlocked the front door, and they entered the house, which had been closed up since the past fall. They would have to rough it, Eddie said, because there wouldn't be any servants in the house until his brother and his family moved in for the summer. The house was two stories, simply finished, with plastered walls, beaded wood ceilings and smooth, unfinished cypress flooring. The top floor had been a dormitory for the students. The kitchen was in a separate building connected by a breezeway. A pipe had been sunk in the ground to reach water, which was hand pumped into the house. Kerosene lamps provided light. This day in May was warm enough to open up the windows and doors to catch the sea breeze. They sat in rocking chairs on the porch and drank whiskey and water, but no ice.

Later, they took a cast net out into the creek behind the island and caught minnows and mullet to use for bait. They rigged two surfcasting rods and reels and walked across the dunes to the hard sand of the beach. A slight east wind curled small breakers toward the shore. It was a three-quarter rising tide, the right time to catch fish. They cast out, beyond the breakers, and waited. In less than five minutes, Abram had a strike. There was a jerk at the end of his pole, and the fish took line from his reel. He jerked back and set the hook. He let the fish take more line but slowly applied more pressure to the reel. He stopped the fish and began to pump the rod and reel in the slack. The fish tried to run again but was too tired to overcome the strain on the hook. In another two minutes, Abram dragged the fish through the surf and up onto the dry sand. It was a beautiful spot-tailed bass of more than ten pounds.

They continued to fish, although the first fish was more than enough to feed them for the rest of the time they would be there. They kept one more that Eddie caught but threw the others back into the surf. It had been a good day. They returned to the house, cleaned, scaled and filleted the fish and sat on the porch with another whiskey. Later, they gathered some driftwood for the stove, started a fire and cooked the fish. They ate rice and beans that they had brought. They sat and talked about the good times that had come back to Georgetown. Eddie said:

> *My father* [Heiman Kaminski] *was born in Prussia in 1839. He came to the United States just in time to get caught up in the Civil War. He joined the Confederate army and served until the end of the war. He had no money when he moved to Georgetown in 1866. He and a partner, another Jew, started a grocery and hardware business. He's a good businessman. Throughout those difficult times of Reconstruction, my father built up his hardware business and invested his money on Wall Street, with the help of relatives in New York. In 1882, as you know, he had the three-masted schooner* Linah C. Kaminski *built in Bath, Maine, and she still sails today, even though he sold her a few years ago. Then he convinced the Clyde Line to start passenger service to Georgetown, and he became their agent. He even started a boat oar factory. Now, he's one of the founders of the new bank in Georgetown. He's provided well for us. All we have to do is keep it going.*

"I've never seen so many ships in Georgetown," said Abram. "If they keep cutting trees at the rate they are going now, I don't see how there will be enough to last very much longer. Then, what will Georgetown do?"

"There are plenty of trees farther up the rivers. If the federal government will give us the money to widen and deepen the Pee Dee and Santee Rivers, finish the locks around the rapids and make the rivers navigable upstream into North Carolina, we can be the biggest port on the Southeast coast. Logs can be floated down the rivers, and farmers will send their cotton and tobacco to Georgetown and we'll ship all over the world. We are already a bigger port than Charleston or Savannah and growing bigger every year."

"Good times don't last forever. New Bedford thought the whaling industry would last forever, but petroleum was discovered and most of the whales were killed. The same thing could happen to Georgetown with trees if they don't replant. New Bedford was saved by the textile industry."

"The whole South is booming. We've got trees and we've got cotton and tobacco. And we've got cheap labor. Before long, we'll have the cotton mills down here rather than sending the cotton up north. Believe me, Abram, the South will rise again. You're in the right place. You should move Lillian and your family back to Georgetown, go into business with us and make a fortune."

Abram thought that he heard liquor talking. "Well, I like what I'm doing pretty well. I'm making enough for Lillian and the girls to be comfortable. I don't think I could stay in one place. You should go with me sometime. I'd let you climb the rigging and shift a topsail."

"No thanks. I'm thinking more about buying a motor yacht. You know, they're making yachts with naptha and gasoline engines now. I read that Charles Flint's yacht, *Arrow*, set a new world's speed record last September going forty-five miles an hour down the Hudson River."

"By the way," Abram said, "did that barber who killed the deputy ever get hanged?"

Funny you should mention that. It was only two weeks ago that Brownfield was finally scheduled to be hanged. He made a final request to have a meeting with Mayor Morgan, J.B. Steele, D.J. Crowley and me. The mayor thought we ought to do it, so we did. Brownfield pleaded with us to allow him to spend the rest of his life in jail but not to hang him. He said that to be hanged would be a big disgrace to his wife and children and that they wouldn't be able to live in the community. I felt sorry for him and wanted to allow him to stay in jail, but Mayor Morgan and the others knew that the deputy's family would never stand for allowing him to live. We turned him down. The day before he was going to be hanged, he took poison in his cell and died. I'm just glad it's over.

Abram and Eddie returned to Georgetown on Sunday. On Monday, a manager at ACL told Abram that the *City of Georgetown* would be loaded with a special cargo of long pine beams to be unloaded in Boston. The beams were going to be used in the construction of a new textile mill at Fall River, Massachusetts. For the rest of the week, lighters tied up at the bow of the *City of Georgetown*. Cranes and blocks and tackle lifted pine beams, as large as sixteen by twenty inches and as long as forty feet, through loading hatches in the bow of the vessel. They were carefully lowered into the bilge, stacked and fastened down. Similar heavy beams were brought out onto the wharf by trams, lifted and swung onto the deck using the booms of the *City of Georgetown* as hoists. This beautiful lumber had been cut from some of the last stands of virgin longleaf pine within fifty miles of Georgetown. The ten-day passage was made in good weather, and they arrived in Boston in late June.

The *City of Georgetown* continued to make fast passages between Georgetown and New York for the remainder of 1903. During the spring of 1904, the *City of Georgetown* made a series of passages to Bridgeport, Connecticut. The following article appeared in the May 4, 1904 issue of the *Georgetown Times*:

> *A dispatch from Bridgeport Conn., to the* New York Herald *says: The four-masted schooner* City of Georgetown, *Capt. J.A. Slocum, reached here last evening with a cargo of yellow pine timber from Georgetown, S.C., just twenty-two days after her clearing from this port. The trip lowers the record by seven days.*
>
> *The* City of Georgetown *cleared April 2, light, for South Carolina, and five days later arrived at Georgetown, having averaged 140 miles a day for the trip of a little more than seven hundred miles. She started on her return trip April 17 and passed a north-bound Mallory steamship, a feat which greatly pleases her master. The round trip has never been in less than thirty days.*

The *City of Georgetown* was loading machinery for Atlantic Coast Lumber Company at Pier 27, almost under the Brooklyn Bridge in New York City, on June 15, 1904, when the 235-foot side-wheel steamer *General Slocum* got underway with over 1,100 passengers from a Lutheran church congregation for an excursion up the East River toward Long Island Sound. About ten o'clock, Abram watched the steamer, named after a Civil War general who was probably one of his distant relatives, glide up the river, aided by a swift current. A band was playing, and people danced as the ship disappeared around a bend. An hour later, sirens were sounding and boats were hurrying up the river toward billowing smoke from a fire that had started aboard the *General Slocum*. People said that the vessel had caught fire and hundreds of people were burning to death or drowning. When the current reversed in the afternoon, bodies began to float down the East River and past the *City of Georgetown*, one lodging against the hull of the schooner. Abram and his crew launched the ship's yawl and helped to pull dead women and children from the water. They were dressed in their best clothes. It was a horrible task to retrieve their charred and bloated bodies. The fire aboard the *General Slocum* was the worst maritime disaster in American history, killing over 1,000 people.

Abram always considered himself lucky to have made so many passages around Cape Hatteras without getting caught by a serious storm. In 1904, more than sixty different three- and four-masted schooners cleared Georgetown, and for a few, it was their last voyage. The 180-foot *Nathan Lawrence* sailed from Georgetown for Bridgeport in September carrying a load of lumber. The *New York Times* reported on September 18:

> *The third shipwrecked crew to be landed in Wilmington since the disastrous hurricane of Tuesday and Wednesday came up to the city yesterday. The rescued men were Capt. E.W. Barlow and seven men, taken from the wreck of the schooner* Nathan Lawrence *in the Gulf Stream, off Cape Romain.*
>
> *The* Nathan Lawrence *sailed from Georgetown, SC last Monday. The hurricane struck the ship at 6 PM Tuesday and carried away every sail, though snugly furled around the booms. Huge seas boarded the ship, swept both lifeboats away, the forward house, the midships house and all the water tanks and belongings of the crew. In the midst of the awful sea, Tuesday, at midnight, the ship sprang a leak, and filled in thirty minutes. Nothing was left above water but the after house, and on this the crew lashed themselves and waited for daylight.*
>
> *At the break of day, Wednesday, the schooner* D.J. Sawyer *sighted the wreck and bore down on it. The sea was too rough all day to allow a boat to be launched, but at 5:30 o'clock in the evening a boat was put over and all hands were saved.*
>
> *The rescuing schooner itself had suffered from the storm, having lost her jib boom, mainsail and two headsails.*

During that same hurricane, the schooner *Emily F. Northam* had sailed from Georgetown, and the *Georgetown Times* reported:

The steamer Chatham *from Savannah, today, reports that last Thursday night, off the South Carolina coast, the three master schooner* Emily F. Northam *of Philadelphia was seen ablaze amidships.*

A strong wind carried showers of sparks from the burning vessel. Her decks were awash, her masts standing, and her burgee still flying, but all her gaffs and booms were gone with exception of main gaff, and her yawl boat was missing.

Captain Hudgins of the Chatham *got as close as safety would permit, but could discover no signs of life aboard, and he believes the crew got away in her yawl. The schooner was lumber laden and may have become water logged in the cyclone Thursday night, the crew setting fire to her before leaving.*

Before the September 1904 hurricane, and whenever other hurricane threats occurred while the *City of Georgetown* was loading at the Port of Georgetown, Abram had his vessel towed away from the Atlantic Coast Lumber wharf and up the Waccamaw River to its most protected spot, Schooner Creek. He dropped both three-thousand-pound anchors, each with fifty fathoms of chain. He removed all canvas and loose gear, and he and the crew stayed on board until the danger had passed.

Abram was pressed by ACL to make more and more frequent passages loaded with lumber. During one voyage to New York, the *City of Georgetown* carried 630,000 board feet of lumber, a new record for four-masted schooners. Abram often made his return voyage without any cargo so that he could start his lumber-laden voyages north even more quickly. Whenever the *City of Georgetown* sailed south at maximum speed and without cargo, she would often be stabilized by a few tons of smooth ballast stones in her hold. When she arrived at the ACL wharf, stevedores unloaded the ballast stone for later use in stabilizing the muddy banks of the Sampit River. There were no natural stones along the coast of South Carolina, which at least made it less dangerous to run aground there than on the rocky coasts of Maine and Massachusetts. The *City of Georgetown* was seldom in any port more than a week. One day in 1904, while the *City of Georgetown* was in port at the ACL wharf, Ex-President Grover Cleveland's yacht, the *Oneida*, tied up behind the *City of Georgetown* and took on a load of coal. The president stepped out on his bow, shouted in Abram's direction, "Splendid vessel," and returned to his cabin. He didn't recognize Abram as the boy who had once chummed his fish bait on Cuttyhunk Island.

The *City of Georgetown* is underway, loaded with lumber on deck. *Courtesy of Maine Maritime Museum.*

Freeman Farr died in March 1905. Abram attended the funeral at Prince George Winyah Episcopal Church, the oldest and most prestigious church in Georgetown. Farr was buried in the Prince George Cemetery. Atlantic Coast Lumber Corporation's management was reorganized, and an aggressive new manager arrived from New York. He demanded that more lumber be shipped while the market was good and the supply of timber lasted. Atlantic Coast Lumber Company had stopped leasing steamships and had bought the steamships *Aragon*, *Katadin* and *Richmond*, which were kept busy hauling lumber. They had even purchased a few old schooners and barques and converted them into schooner barges, which were loaded with lumber and towed in tandem to their destinations by oceangoing steam tugs. The idea was disgusting to Abram. Schooners like the *City of Georgetown* were being given last priority in the loading of lumber.

For his part, Abram set another schooner speed record in March 1905 by sailing from New York to Georgetown, port to port, in just three days. It was one of those few perfect passages. The *City of Georgetown* sailed out of New York with no cargo, riding high. The wind was a steady twenty-five knots on the starboard beam. Abram had his best crew—his regular experienced mate and engineer, three Norwegians and a Greek sailor. He ordered all sails set—lowers, topsails and headsails—and they stayed set from beginning to end. When they were up to speed, the log registered twelve knots. Abram couldn't believe it. They stayed east of the Gulf Stream and made few course changes. The wind stayed steady and on their beam. During the second day, Abram spotted a steamship far ahead, heading in their same direction. By noon, they had caught up with a two-hundred-foot steamship spewing out its maximum amount of smoke, trying not to be overtaken. Abram's crew laughed and yelled at the steamship as the *City of Georgetown* passed close on its port side, slowly pulling away. By nightfall, the steamship was barely visible behind them. The third day, they passed Cape Fear. Seventy-two hours after clearing New York, the *City of Georgetown* was anchored in front of Georgetown Lighthouse.

Although Abram wasn't given much credit by the managers of ACL, he was a hero to many sailors and other captains who envied his accomplishments and his refusal to accept steamships as replacements for sail. He had the best crew of any schooner and a waiting list of sailors who wanted to sail with him. In 1905, Abram was forty-four years old and at his prime as a sailor and a man. He enjoyed his fame and the attention given to him. He drank with his crew, but he could also entertain the most important men of Georgetown. Georgetown was a wide-open town, with enough bars and bawdyhouses to serve the several hundred sailors who were in Georgetown at any one time.

On December 19, 1905, Abram and his first mate sat on the stern of the *City of Georgetown* and watched Georgetown's Centennial Marine Parade of almost fifty vessels—including the U.S. Navy monitor warships *Nevada* and *Arkansas*—pass in a double line up the Sampit River, past jubilant crowds along the Front Street waterfront. Abram had American flags run up to the peak of each topmast of the *City of Georgetown*, as had all the other ships in port. The city on the Sampit had gone all out to celebrate the 100th anniversary of its incorporation. There had been street parades and speeches by the governor and other politicians during the entire day. Abram thought that Mayor Morgan had outdone himself this time with such an elaborate celebration of Georgetown's prosperity. Abram wondered how much longer this frenzy, based on cutting down all the trees in the South, could go on.

Crowds along Georgetown's waterfront during the centennial boat parade of December 1905. *Courtesy of Georgetown County Digital Library.*

The year 1906 started with a bang. New York Stock Exchange averages were the highest in history. The federal government was completing a large and elaborate customs house and post office building in Georgetown to handle the increased amount of shipping. However, by summer, for some reason, demand for lumber in the Northeast began to level off. The three steamships of ACL continued to be loaded with lumber to make passages from Georgetown to the Northeast, but the *City of Georgetown* sat idle in August, waiting for cargo. Finally, in September, there was an order, the schooner was loaded and she made ready to get underway for Philadelphia.

On September 14, a steam tug towed the *City of Georgetown* through Winyah Bay with the pilot onboard. As they approached the jetties, Abram looked at the sky and a falling barometer, and he didn't like what he saw. He told the pilot that if this passage weren't his only chance to make a profit all summer, he would order the ship to turn back and wait for this weather system to pass. He knew it was the height of hurricane season.

"Are you sure you want to start this passage now? I don't like the look of it either," the pilot said.

Abram replied, "It's coming up from the south. It's probably way east of us and will turn more out to sea, like most of them do. I'll keep to the western edge of the Gulf Stream and go up the Cape Fear River if it looks worse. You had better get back to shore."

The sea was fairly calm. Long, oily swells washed over the rocks of the jetties as the schooner passed over the bar. Winds were light from the east as the donkey engine hoisted the four lower sails. Abram ordered up the topsails and headsails, and they were making six knots as night approached. When they reached the edge of the Gulf Stream, the east wind had picked up to twenty-five knots. Ocean swells were higher and longer but not breaking. The barometer continued to fall. They shortened sail before nightfall. The *City of Georgetown* passed within sight of Frying Pan Shoals Light during the night.

When morning came, the wind began to back toward the northeast and increase. The barometer was dropping fast. Abram knew they were in for trouble. He knew he shouldn't have started. He had always prided himself on being cautious. Now, he had no choice but to get around Hatteras and duck into Norfolk. He ordered the mate to further reduce sail and point up as much as he could, but it wasn't possible to keep to their intended course. Waves in the Gulf Stream were much higher and steeper, and some were breaking over the port bow. It began to rain. The storm was catching up with them. He knew it would pass east of them on its northeasterly course, but he couldn't tell how close. They would soon be east of the Gulf Stream, but their course would lead them toward the storm. All lower sails had been struck, and only a reefed jib and one topsail remained as winds reached fifty knots. Waves broke heavily against the starboard side of the vessel and washed across the lumber stored on deck. The ship heeled over to port, pitched up to meet oncoming waves and then plunged down. The sky was almost black, with heavy rain. Wind moaned through the rigging, shrieking when there was a gust. Abram thought how much worse it would have been if he hadn't insisted that the ship have a wheelhouse. They weren't dry there, but there was some protection for the two men at the wheel. Abram cursed himself. Everything had been going right for him until now. He had made a bad decision and was going to pay for it. He watched his ship—the ship he had built and sailed at record speeds—being pounded before his eyes. He had to come through this storm, repair whatever damage there was and get back to normal.

They were approaching the latitude of Cape Hatteras when part of the starboard deck load of lumber broke loose. Two chains snapped, and boards flew everywhere. The two steersmen fought to hold the wheel. The spanker boom, which had been securely tied down, parted a line and swung across the roof of the aft cabin, crashing into the port shrouds. The steersmen couldn't hold the heading, and the schooner broached into a trough between two breakers, heeling the schooner over so much that she almost capsized. The spanker mast shook from the blow of the boom. The spanker topmast gave way and crashed on top of the wheelhouse. It slid aft and struck the ship's yawl, carrying it away. The next waves broke across the entire deck, washing away more of the deck load of lumber. Some of the boards bashed against the booms and shredded the furled lower sails.

Abram shouted for the helmsmen to turn downwind. He ran to help them. The ship turned slowly downwind so that waves rolled in and broke over the stern. Abram estimated the wind velocity at more than eighty knots and the wave heights at close to forty feet. He had three men in the wheelhouse. The engineer and another man were forward trying to keep the pump going. He wasn't sure where his other men were, and there was no way a man could move from bow to stern without being washed overboard. The engineer reported that the below-deck cargo was holding fast but there was over four feet of water in the hold. The donkey engine pump wasn't keeping up with the water coming through the hull.

The *City of Georgetown* was making six knots downwind under bare poles, rolling to her rails. As the center of the storm came closer, the ever-stronger wind shrieked through the rigging above the superstructure of the schooner. Rain fell in torrents. The wind's fury increased. The seas became mountainous. Tops of huge waves were blown off to mingle with the rain and fill the air with water. Objects at a short distance weren't visible. Abram heard another crash on deck and saw the mizzen topmast fall onto the port rail, splinter it and go overboard. *My God*, Abram thought, *are we going to make it through this?* For one of the first times in his life, he felt fear. He thought of Lillian, Florence and Marjorie. Would he see them again? He felt despair for just a moment and then forced himself to plan their next move.

As the second night fell, the wind began to subside. It was easier to hold the wheel, but it was harder to see from which direction waves were approaching. Waves were still twenty feet high, lifting the stern and rolling the ship thirty degrees one way and then the other. When a wave passed under the keel, the stern slid down into a trough and the bow pointed at the sky. Abram relieved the man at the wheel, using his skill to feel the approaching waves and steer to keep from broaching. None of the crew had slept in two nights, but there was no relief. Abram began to feel a numbness, a dullness inside of his head, a feeling he had never experienced.

Before dawn, the sky had cleared and there was a moon and stars above. A pink dawn showed them big swells but less than forty knots of southeast wind. The barometer was up. Later, Abram forced himself to take a sunshot. He estimated they were almost east and slightly north of Norfolk, about fifty miles out. He surveyed the damage. There was no way they could sail. The jib boom was split and hanging loose. Two topmasts were gone. The spanker boom was broken. The sails had been ripped and shredded. The worst problem was rising water in the bilge. Pounding had opened seams in the hull, and the hold was filling. *The ship probably won't go to the bottom because of the buoyancy of the wood in the hold,* Abram thought. At the rate they were sinking, the decks would be awash before nightfall. If the hull sank too far, they would have to throw the rest of the deck lumber overboard to keep the top-heavy ship from capsizing. Abram ordered distress signals to be deployed. The men gathered around the aft cabin and waited.

In the afternoon, a lookout spotted the smoke of a steamship in the distance. The ship came closer, and when a wave lifted the *City of Georgetown*, Abram could make out a small steamer running out of Norfolk. Its course would bring it close enough to see the *Cit of Georgetown*. When the steamer was less than a mile away, it altered course and steamed straight toward them. It stopped less than one hundred yards away. The name on the stern was *Carl Menzel*, from Hamburg, Germany. The vessel launched a boat, which motored close to the stern of the *City of Georgetown*. Waves were still too high to try to come aboard. A sailor dressed as an officer yelled toward Abram, "Do you seek assistance?" Abram shouted back, "We do."

The launch motored back to the steamer. The steamer positioned itself about one hundred yards ahead of the *City of Georgetown*. The launch loaded the end of a thick hawser, which was connected to the stern of the steamer, and motored to the side of the schooner. A sailor stood up in the launch and threw a monkey fist on the end of a small line over the rail of the schooner. The crew of the schooner hauled the hawser on board and fastened it securely to a Samson post in the bow. The launch returned to the *Carl Menzel* and was loaded aboard. The steamer tightened the hawser and began to tow the waterlogged *City of Georgetown* slowly toward Norfolk. Twenty-four hours later, the wreck of the *City of Georgetown* was tied up alongside a pier of a repair yard in Norfolk. An article in the October 12, 1906 Columbia *State* newspaper read:

> *The four-masted schooner* City of Georgetown, *which was rendered almost a total wreck in the gale of Sept. 17, is now lying at the wharf at Norfolk, Va., full of water. The tramp steamer which towed her in claimed $12,000 salvage, which being refused by the owners, the vessel was libeled for $25,000. The matter will be carried into the courts. In the meantime, the vessel will be put under bond, and repairs begun. She will then proceed to her destination with the cargo of lumber, part of the deckload of which, however, was lost.*

As soon as the *City of Georgetown* was tied up, Abram climbed down a ladder onto the wharf and examined the outside of the schooner. He was devastated by the amount of damage. The captain of the *Carl Menzel* told Abram that he had contacted the owner of his ship, who would bring a salvage document to Captain Slocum the next day. Meanwhile, he said, he must be on his way to New York, and he left. Abram telegraphed his owners' agent in New Bedford and briefly outlined the damage to the schooner, saying that the crew was all right and that he would pay them off. He sent another telegram to Lillian saying that the damaged schooner was in Norfolk, he and the rest of the crew were all right and he would have to stay there until arrangements for repairs had been made. He told her he would be home as soon as he could. He spoke with the manager of the repair yard and asked for a list of damages and repair estimates. More pumps had been put aboard to empty the hold, but the schooner would have to be put into drydock to repair the hull. Abram went to a bank and paid off the men. He gave them money for transportation to their homes. He thanked them for their bravery and said he would contact them when the schooner was repaired. Abram climbed back aboard the *City of Georgetown*, entered his soaked and wrecked stateroom, recovered a bottle of whiskey from a drawer, opened it and took a swig from the bottle. Soaking wet books lay all over his cabin. He picked up his valuable but ruined volume of *Bowditch Practical Navigator*, put it down, stretched out on his wet mattress and slept for twelve hours.

What the *City of Georgetown* had been through was more than a gale. It was a major hurricane that had roared up the East Coast, spreading devastation in its path. Another schooner that regularly called at Georgetown, the *Nellie Floyd*, was wrecked and sunk by the storm.

Her captain and crew were picked out of a lifeboat by another vessel. Georgetown had not been spared. The rice fields on the banks of the rivers above Georgetown were flooded by a storm surge, and the crops were lost, making a final end to rice growing in Georgetown. Pawleys Island homes were damaged or destroyed, and the railroad that Atlantic Coast Lumber Company had built from Pawleys Island to Hagley Landing was destroyed. Smokestacks and equipment at the ACL mill and other mills in Georgetown had been destroyed.

After a frustrating week of arranging matters with the repair yard and meeting lawyers for the *Carl Menzel*, Abram was able to go home. Lillian had thanked God that Abram had survived the storm. *He might not be so lucky next time*, she thought. She hoped he wouldn't go back to sea. She told him that he should quit the sailing business and go into steamships or quit altogether and get a job in Somerville, but she knew he wasn't listening. He seemed more concerned about repairing and getting the ship ready to go than about her feelings.

Abram was called to a meeting of the owners of the *City of Georgetown* in New Bedford. Quite a few of the fifty owners attended, although none was from Georgetown. The purpose was to determine what assessment would be necessary to repair the vessel and settle the salvage lawsuit. All the owners had been pleased by a 10 percent return on their investment ever since the *City of Georgetown* was commissioned, but now they had to return part of that money. They didn't blame Abram for what had happened to the schooner in the storm. Damage to schooners in the lumber trade from storms was a common occurrence, and part of the damage repair would be covered by insurance. They left the meeting with hopes that Abram would see to it that repairs were made quickly so that the schooner could go back to work, making them more money.

Abram spent most of the next nine months getting the *City of Georgetown* repaired and the lawsuit settled. Finally, Abram had her ready to sail back to Georgetown. Before Abram left Somerville, Lillian again pleaded with him to give up seafaring and take a position on shore. Abram listened, but he could think of no other life that he was fit for. He promised Lillian that he would try to find something else once this voyage was over.

Abram made ready to get underway for Georgetown. He was less sure of himself than before the storm and acted more cautiously. He hesitated to socialize and tell sea stories with his men. He had no trouble putting together another crew. No one blamed him for what had happened to the *City of Georgetown*. When the schooner arrived in Georgetown and was tied up at the ACL wharf, he was greeted as an old friend by other captains, their crews and the storekeepers along Front Street. Eddie Kaminski came to see him, and they reminisced and drank rum at the Red Store Tavern.

The next day, Abram was ordered to the office of Rufus Barnes, the son-in-law of Freeman Farr and a manager of ACL. Abram and Rufus had never gotten along. Rufus told him that because of a banking crisis in New York, the lumber business was terrible. The stock market had lost 40 percent of its value. There was less demand for lumber, and two of the sawmills were being shut down for lack of orders. The three steamships that the company owned were idle part of the time. Freight rates were down, and ACL would no longer lease the *City of Georgetown* at the high rate. The lumber being loaded aboard the *City of Georgetown* was the last order from ACL. ACL's lease of the *City of Georgetown* was cancelled, based on the fact that the schooner hadn't been able to fulfill its obligation to haul lumber since the storm of 1906. He ended the conversation by sympathizing with the Georgetown owners of Abram's schooner, saying that the days of sailing ships were over. On July 1, 1907, the *City of Georgetown* sailed with lumber from the port of Georgetown, South Carolina, for the last time.

Chapter 6

The Last Days of
the *City of Georgetown*

(1907–1914)

The passage from Georgetown to New York was slow. There was little wind, and what there was blew from the wrong direction. If it hadn't been for the Gulf Stream, it would have taken them the rest of the summer to get there. The crew spent a lot of time fishing. Abram stood long hours outside his cabin, depressed and looking out to sea, wondering if and when the ship's agent would be able to find cargo. When Abram had contacted him, he had been very disappointed and had said that it would be impossible to haul lumber at the reduced rate and make a profit. He had nothing and suggested that Abram, after unloading cargo in New York, sail to New Bedford and lay up there until a contract was found. Abram thought of the owners of the ship and their disappointment. He was a ¾₄ owner himself. He was sure they would love to sell their interest in the *City of Georgetown*, but there would be no buyers.

When the *City of Georgetown* was tied up along a wharf in New Bedford, Abram paid off the crew, arranged for ship security and returned home to Somerville. Lillian was happy to have Abram at home. She and the girls loved their time with him. Abram and Lillian discussed, among other things, their money problems. Nothing would be coming in until the ship had another contract. They would have to use some of their savings and be more frugal with their spending. Abram spoke vaguely about retiring and starting some business. Lillian encouraged him to do so, but he took no action to find other work. Lillian knew he longed to be back at sea. Abram kept in touch with the ship's agent, but he was unable to find a profitable cargo contract for the rest of the year.

While Abram continued to wait for his agent to find a cargo contract, he repaired everything around the house that Lillian told him about. He played with Marjorie and was a good husband, but he yearned to be back at sea. Finally, in March 1908, he received a telegram telling him that there was good news. The agent had signed a five-year contract with International Salt Company of New York for the *City of Georgetown* to deliver bulk salt from Bridgeport to Savannah. Also, there was a good chance that return passages from Savannah to New York could be made, hauling poles for power and telephone lines. When Abram told Lillian, she said she was sorry he was going back to sea. She was tired of his being away so much and having to worry about him while he was gone. Oh yes, she admitted, they could use the money it would bring in, but if he really loved her, he would find a job where he could live at home. Abram wasn't listening.

Abram left Somerville the next day for New Bedford and arrived about noon. He walked down to the wharf, where the *City of Georgetown* was laid up. She was a sad sight. Her paint was peeling and the gold leaf fading from her billetheads. He climbed a ladder to her deck and opened up the aft cabin. It was cold and damp inside. Everything was as he had left it. Within a few days, the crew arrived and began to bring the vessel back to the condition that Abram demanded.

The *City of Georgetown* began a long series of trips between Bridgeport and Savannah. They sometimes hauled cotton instead of poles to the North. Occasionally, the cargo was coal instead of salt, heading south. Abram was happy again, feeling the wind in the sails of his schooner and matching his wits against the weather. There was less pressure on him than when he had sailed for Atlantic Coast Lumber Company. Abram began to replace his library onboard the schooner. He was able to decide for himself whether to delay a passage because of pending bad weather. There were still times when the barometer dropped and the wind and waves increased after he was well underway, but he was careful to reduce sail and detour away from pending storms, even if it meant adding extra miles and days to the passage. He felt he had a good crew, most of whom stayed with him voyage after voyage. There was never an opportunity to sail into Georgetown, although he heard that it was still one of the busiest lumber ports. He understood that most of the lumber was being delivered by steamship.

Abram was able to spend more time between passages at home. In 1909, Abram and Lillian attended Florence's wedding in New Bedford. Abram enjoyed a reunion with his family, including Lydia, Myra and Frederick. More time passed. Abram spent the Christmas holiday of 1912 in Somerville. The *City of Georgetown* was tied up in New York City.

That winter was very cold. When Abram returned to the schooner in January, there was a foot of snow on the ground, and temperatures were well below freezing. The rigging of the *City of Georgetown* was coated in ice. Snow covered the decks. Abram's steward had known he was coming and had stoked the coal fire in the heater of Abram's cabin. Abram had a headache and a cold and didn't feel like doing much besides lying in his bed. He wondered how many more years he would be doing this. Abram had chosen his life's work—risk and discomfort traded for the freedom and contentment of the sea. He guessed it had been worth it, but there were times—like now, when it was zero degrees and he was supposed to make a midwinter passage to Savannah—when he would rather be doing something else.

For the next week, it was too cold for the stevedores to load salt into the hold of the *City of Georgetown*. The crew returned to the schooner, unhappy and grumbling about the cold passage that lay ahead. Abram's mate, Johnson, had made many passages with him. He was a stoic man and a good sailor. He managed to get the others moving, readying the ship to get underway. The ship's cook, the only black man in the crew, stayed close to the galley stove to keep warm. The engineer, Petersen, was a Norwegian with over twenty years of experience in dealing with Hyde Donkey Engines. Two of the able seamen, Olsen and Jacobsen, were also Norwegian and had made several passages on the *City of Georgetown*. Antonio Malmberg was a first-class seaman from another schooner who had agreed to make the passage. The other seaman was new to the ship, signed on by a labor contractor in New York.

Abram dealt with the contractors who provisioned the schooner. Abram always planned to provision for thirty days, even though he hadn't had a passage that long in several years. He gave notice to the tugboat contractor and the port pilot that they would be ready to go by February 1. He telephoned Lillian, saying that he wasn't looking forward to this passage but weather predictions were good, and he should be in Savannah by the end of the first week in February. He wished Marjorie a happy twelfth birthday.

All the salt had been stowed below and the three hatches covered and sealed by the last day of January. In the mid-morning of February 1, 1913, a tug nudged the *City of Georgetown* away from the pier and into the East

River. The temperature was just below twenty degrees. All of the crew wore their heaviest oilskins and sou'westers. They were towed out through the Ambrose Channel, past Sandy Hook and into the ocean. The weather was clear, with a steady twenty-knot northwest wind. Abram ordered all lower sails raised by the donkey engine, plus the jib and forestaysail. They made good speed and, by nightfall, were halfway to Cape May, the southern tip of New Jersey. Abram ordered the spanker lowered. The *City of Georgetown* was on a starboard tack, heading southwest. Abram had the 8:00 p.m. to midnight watch, along with Olsen at the wheel and the new man as lookout on the bow. As midnight neared, Abram could see the faint flashes of Five Fathom Bank lightship ahead, due east of and marking the entrance to Delaware Bay.

Johnson, the mate, relieved Abram as officer of the watch at midnight. Before Abram left the deck, he checked the port and starboard navigation lanterns. Satisfied that they were burning brightly, he went below to his cabin. When Johnson took over, he automatically looked in all directions for ship traffic. The intersection of the Delaware Bay ship channel, where ships from Philadelphia and Wilmington entered the ocean and met the main north–south ocean lane, was often a busy place, which was why the lightship was there. When Johnson looked toward the west, he thought he saw in the distance a faint white steaming light of an approaching vessel. He warned Malmberg, who had taken over as lookout, to watch the approaching light carefully. Johnson watched the light to make sure its bearing relative to the *City of Georgetown* changed as time passed, which meant the vessel would pass behind or ahead of the schooner. As the approaching vessel came closer, its bearing wasn't changing. By then, Johnson could see other lights high up on the vessel, meaning it was probably a large ocean liner coming out of Philadelphia. Johnson told Malmberg to check their green starboard navigation light to make sure the liner could see it and would change its course to avoid the *City of Georgetown*. The lights on the liner were getting brighter, fast, and still the bearing didn't change. Johnson was becoming alarmed, and he grabbed an electric torch from beside the binnacle, turned it on and shined it onto the mainsail. *They must see us,* he thought. *They must make a turn soon.* He yelled down to Abram's cabin, saying to come quickly.

It was 0050, fifty minutes after midnight. The sky was clear, with stars overhead, wind steady from the northwest and the temperature twenty degrees. They were heading southwest. The schooner *City of Georgetown* was less than a half mile east of the bright flashes of Five Fathom Bank lightship.

A comparison of the relative sizes of the *City of Georgetown* and the *Prinz Oskar. Courtesy of Maine Maritime Museum.*

The huge bulk of the ocean liner was bearing down on them. Abram told the helmsman to hold the course steady, which was the law. The vessel under sail has the right of way; all seamen know that rule. The liner had to turn. Why hadn't it turned or even slowed its speed, which Abram estimated to be about twelve knots? Johnson again shined the torch on the sails, but he knew it was too late. The bow of the liner loomed fifty feet above the schooner. Abram's last order to the helmsman was to throw over the wheel to starboard. He yelled to cut the sails loose.

The bow-to-bow collision occurred at 0055. The jib boom and bowsprit of the *City of Georgetown* struck the side of the liner's steel bow like a battering ram. The impact aboard the *City of Georgetown* was like an explosion. Everyone was thrown forward onto the deck, crashing into walls or rails. The noise of splintering wood and snapping cables was horrific. The masts had strained forward at the impact. Before Abram could recover, he heard the cracking of the mast beside him. He looked up and watched in horror as all four masts bent back, broke off ten feet above the deck and crashed onto the roofs of the deckhouses. Sails, booms, topmasts, gaffs and rigging made a tangled mass on the deck. Abram stood, staring forward and up at a black steel hull. For a minute, the two vessels were locked together. Then, Abram could feel the throb of the liner's engines. *What is happening?*

he thought. The liner was backing up, for a moment pulling the *City of Georgetown* with it. Abram watched as the two powerful reverse engines of the liner tore the bow from the schooner, opening a huge hole in her wooden hull. The *City of Georgetown* began to tilt forward as water rushed into the bow of the ship.

Abram, Johnson, Malmberg and Petersen ran aft, climbing over wreckage to reach the ship's yawl, which, amazingly, still hung from davits at the stern. Already, the schooner was listing forward. They loosened the lines holding the yawl, and it dropped toward the heaving sea. Abram could see three of the other four crewmen trying to climb toward the stern. He yelled for them to jump over the side. Abram and the other three in the yawl managed to push clear of the sinking schooner and started to row toward the cook and steward, who were in the water, close to the starboard side. They gasped for breath as they were pulled from the freezing water. They spotted a third man, close off the stern, and pulled him in. By then, the bow was far underwater with the stern pointing at the sky. As the bow sank, whirlpools of water surrounded it. Abram saw his last man, who had been asleep in the fo'c'sle, climb the slanting deck to the stern and dive into the sea. The yawl reached him just before swirling waters pulled him under.

The liner had launched two of her lifeboats, but all of the schooner's crew were in the yawl. As they rowed toward a ladder along the liner's starboard side, Abram read the name *Prinz Oskar*, Hamburg, Germany. Some of the German crew helped Abram and the rest of the wet and freezing crew of the *City of Georgetown* onto the deck of the liner. None of them was seriously injured. Abram watched the stern of his schooner sink into the ocean. He slumped onto the deck of the *Prinz Oskar* and closed his eyes.

Captain Von Leuenfels of the *Prinz Oskar* ordered that the captain and crew of the *City of Georgetown* be given the best of care as the liner limped back toward Delaware Bay. Captain Leuenfels and the other German officers spoke broken English and apologized for the collision. The captain did not admit responsibility for the accident and tried not to discuss details of the accident with Captain Slocum. However, Abram barely hid his anger from the captain and continued to question how any ship with competent officers could make such an error. Finally, the German captain excused himself and turned the care of Captain Slocum over to a steward. The steward told Abram that the bowsprit and one of the anchors of the *City of Georgetown* had penetrated the steel hull of the *Prinz Oskar*. The *Prinz Oskar*'s port anchor and an anchor from the schooner had crashed into the fo'c'sle cabin where he was sleeping and had shattered ice all over him. He said the passengers were frightened by the collision, and some had been thrown from their bunks. Many of them had run upstairs to the upper deck in panic. There were no injuries, but the ship was taking on water and listing. They would discharge their passengers and cargo and return to Philadelphia for repairs.

Abram managed to telegraph from the *Prinz Oskar* to the *City of Georgetown*'s agent to tell him what had happened. Abram asked him to send a telegram to Lillian to let her know that he and the rest of the crew were safe. About noon, Abram and his crew were put ashore with the liner's passengers at Gloucester. The schooner's agent wired money to Abram to pay off the crew and transport them to their homes. Abram had lost everything but the clothes on his back. The log, his sextant, all of his library and personal effects had gone to the bottom. Abram had managed to learn some information about the *Prinz Oskar*, which was owned by the Hamburg-American Lines. He knew there would be a lawsuit, and he looked forward to testifying.

After Abram had bought new clothes and was waiting in the station for a train to take him to Somerville, he read an account of the collision in the *Philadelphia Enquirer*. It was obviously written from the standpoint of those on the *Prinz Oskar*. The article blamed the powerful glare from the Five Fathom Bank lightship, blinding the liner's lookout and causing the disaster. Captain Von Leuenfels said he was on the bridge when the accident occurred, and had it not been for the glare of the lightship, the schooner could have been seen miles away. He was quoted as saying, "When we first sighted the schooner, as we veered away from the lightship, she was not a quarter of a mile away, and apparently every sail was set. I instantly rang off speed and ordered reverse. I saw that the schooner could not take in sail quick enough to stop, nor could she veer away." The article gave Captain Von Leuenfels credit for launching his lifeboats to save the schooner's crew and for calming his own frightened passengers. Abram did verify that the *City of Georgetown* sank in the center of the path of navigation. The article said that the steamer *Essex* reported by wireless on February 2 that it passed a sunken schooner near Five Fathom Bank lightship with foretopmast showing above water. The steamer *West Point*, from London, reported on February 3 that the sunken schooner *City of Georgetown* lay about three-quarters of a mile southeast from Five Fathom Bank Lightship, with one topmast showing above water. Abram folded the newspaper and sank into depression.

When Abram reached home, Lillian and Marjorie did all they could to comfort him. Lillian delayed giving Abram an ultimatum that he must either give up the sea or give up his wife. Abram received many telegrams from friends, sailors, other captains and people he didn't know offering their condolences and blaming the German ship for the disaster. The *Georgetown Times* picked up the story from the *New York Times* and reprinted part of it. It had been years since the *City of Georgetown* had visited Georgetown, but many of its citizens sent letters of condolence. Eddie Kaminski wrote later in the year, saying that 1913 had been a bad year for Georgetown in more ways than one. Not only had they lost the finest four-masted schooner ever built, but also there was a fire at Atlantic Coast Lumber Company that burned up more than half of its sawmill.

Representatives of the other owners of the schooner and the owners of the cargo contacted him about filing suit against Hamburg-American Lines and the *Prinz Oskar*'s officers. A date was set for a meeting with the attorneys to give testimony about the collision. Meanwhile, Abram had no ship and no way to earn an income. Lillian offered to go back to work, but Abram refused to consider that. He promised he would look for a job in the shipping industry while he waited for the results of the lawsuit, which was being delayed by tactics of the German owners of the *Prinz Oskar*.

Abram replied to an ad in the *New York Times* "Help Wanted" section for a customs inspector in Camden, New Jersey. Lillian begged him to take the job. The pay was reasonable, so Abram accepted the offer, which meant that he and his family would have to move to Camden. Lillian was willing to do anything to have a stable and less dangerous home life with Abram. They found an apartment to rent but kept their house in Somerville.

Before starting the new job, Abram, along with the rest of his crew, gave testimony to the attorneys of both sides at a district court in Pennsylvania. Abram thought that their testimony proved that the officers of the *Prinz Oskar* were at fault. However, arguments by the attorneys for the *Prinz Oskar* included the statement, "It is urged by the respondent that the testimony of the officers of the *Prinz Oskar*, by reason of their superior position, education, and training should have greater weight than that of the master, mate and lookout upon the schooner, who not only by reason of their belonging to a different walk of life, but also because of their interest in the outcome of the suit, were less likely to tell the truth." Abram couldn't believe the arrogance of the German officers of the *Prinz Oskar* and their many lawyers. They accused Abram and his crew of lying about the fact that the navigation lights of the *City of Georgetown* were burning at all. They tried to shift the entire blame for the collision to Abram. Captain Von Leuenfels arrived in a starched white uniform, his blonde hair slicked back. He gave the most condemning testimony, knowing that he would lose his job if the *Prinz Oskar* was ruled at fault. At the end of Leuenfels's cross-examination, Abram rose from his seat and started toward him, intending to punch him in the nose, but he was held back. When the day was over, it was stated that the case would not be ruled on by a judge until sometime in 1914. *How could they take so long?* Abram wondered. It was obvious that the Germans were at fault. He worried that their big corporation and slick lawyers would have some influence on the judge's decision. He felt helpless to do anything about it.

Abram started his job in the customs house in Camden in June 1913. From the beginning, he didn't like the work or his boss. He was bored, unchallenged, restless and overqualified. He had never worked for anyone except the captain of a ship, who knew what he was doing. Abram was used to being his own boss. The man he worked for was a bureaucrat who only cared about protecting his own job until he could retire with a pension. Abram tried to go home at night and be a good husband and father, but in spite of his efforts, he found himself longing to get back on the ocean. He spent hours talking with the captains of ships he was inspecting, swapping sea stories with them. Despite his promises to Lillian, he wanted another ship.

In early January 1914, he met the captain of an old four-masted schooner that was tied up in Camden awaiting cargo. The captain of the *Levi S. Andrews* said he was fed up, tired of waiting and didn't like it that the owners' agent wouldn't advance him any money for maintenance of the ship. He said he was going to quit and find another ship. Abram looked the ship over and didn't think she looked so bad. A few days later, without telling Lillian, he contacted the *Andrews*'s owners' agent and applied to replace the previous captain, who had already resigned. Abram's credentials and experience were far above those of the previous captain, although there was still a cloud over his head until the court's decision about the sinking of the *City of Georgetown* was made. The agent offered Abram temporary command of the *Andrews* for her next voyage. He told Abram that he had a contract for the *Andrews* to haul a cargo of coal from Norfolk to Savannah but the ship must leave Camden by the end of the following day and sail to Norfolk. Abram knew he shouldn't accept the job without discussing it with Lillian. He thought about it for another minute, accepted the job as captain and quit his job as customs inspector the same day.

When he arrived home and told Lillian what he had done, she was furious. She said she was leaving him and going back to Somerville with Marjorie. She said she couldn't live with Abram anymore. He had given up a perfectly good job and a stable home life to do the same crazy things he had done before. If he was going to sea again, he could do it without a family. He was selfish and had no concern for her feelings. She started to cry, went into the bedroom and slammed the door.

Abram wanted things to be like they were before, when he was captain of the *City of Georgetown*, when times were good and Lillian accepted the kind of life he had always led. He didn't know what to do to convince Lillian that everything would be okay. He walked down the block to a bar and drank alone. He returned to their house late that night to apologize and beg forgiveness. Lillian and Marjorie were gone. He had another drink and fell asleep.

The next morning, Abram asked his neighbors if they had seen Lillian leave. No one had seen her. He telephoned a neighbor in Somerville, but there was no answer. Abram almost called the agent to quit, but he couldn't make himself do it. The agent had signed on a crew, and Abram was to meet them at the *Andrews* and get ready to sail in ballast from Camden to Norfolk. On the evening of January 20, the *Andrews*, with A.J. Slocum as captain, was towed into the channel and set sail for Norfolk. Once at sea, Abram tried to forget his personal problems and concentrate on his duties as captain. The mate, who had sailed on the *Andrews* before, had been able to manage the raising of the lower sails with their crew of rummies and green hands.

The schooner had been built in Thomaston, Maine, in 1881, which made her almost as old as the *Warren B. Potter*. Her hull leaked enough to require the donkey engine to run her bilge pump all the time. The following day, the *Andrews* sailed close to Five Fathom Bank lightship. Abram stared down into the depths, imagining he saw the wreck of his *City of Georgetown* on the bottom, one hundred feet below. With a favorable wind, the *Levi S. Andrews* was approaching Norfolk on January 22. While Abram was below, the mate steered too close to shore and ran the schooner aground near Wachapreague, Virginia. Abram was forced to seek help from the Wachapreague Life-Saving Station to pull the schooner off. The *Andrews* was finally towed into Norfolk, leaking more than ever.

Abram notified the agent that the *Andrews*'s bottom would have to be repaired. He wrote a note of thanks to Keeper John W. Richardson of the Wachapreague Life-Saving Station, without whose help the *Levi S. Andrews* would probably have been pounded to pieces on the bottom:

> *Dear Sir and Friends: I want to extend our most sincere thanks to you and the men of your station for the courteous treatment we received while my vessel, the schooner* Levi S. Andrews, *was ashore near your station on the 22nd. The owners also join me in this expression of appreciation of your valuable assistance in floating the schooner.*
> *Yours very truly,*
> *A.J. Slocum, Master*

Abram tried to telephone Lillian in Camden and Somerville but was not able to reach her. During his first passage on the *Andrews*, he had begun to have second thoughts. Besides the rot, leaks and an incompetent crew, he had no feeling for the ship. She was more than a little hogged, and she was slow. His bed was lumpy, and he had no library of books to read. He knew he had made a mistake and that this would be his last voyage on the *Levi S. Andrews*.

But that wasn't his only problem. He looked back on his life, a kind of life that was fast disappearing. He had gone to sea during the last days of wooden sailing ships. For a few years, he had been lucky enough to experience adventure and freedom, sailing and matching his strength and wits against the power of the sea. Also, he had helped some of the best craftsmen in the world build a graceful, beautiful wooden sailing schooner. He had sailed her skillfully until that goddamned steel steamship had rammed him. Now, those German bastards were trying to blame him for the accident. The world had changed. Steam engines and steel ships had replaced wooden sailing ships. There would be no turning back. Big corporations controlled the way things were done. Machines had replaced the skills and crafts of human effort. Abram despaired that there was no place for people who even thought like he did.

He wanted to be back at home with Lillian and Marjorie. He loved Lillian more than anything. He would quit the ship when he got to Savannah, go back and find Lillian, make up with her and be a good husband for the rest of his life. But what would he do? He sank into depression, feeling his life was over.

After two weeks of delays, the schooner was ready to leave Norfolk. Abram remembered a life insurance premium that he was supposed to have paid but had forgotten. He wrote out a check for ten dollars and mailed it to the deputy customs inspector in Georgetown, which was where the insurance company was located. He asked that the paid receipt be sent to him in Savannah. On February 20, Abram and the *Levi S. Andrews* departed Norfolk. Winds were up, and the barometer was falling.

On March 28, 1914, this article appeared in the *Georgetown Times*:

> *CAPT. SLOCUM'S SCHOONER LOST?*
> *Considerable interest is felt in local shipping circles with respect to the possible, even probable fate of Capt. A.J. Slocum and his schooner, the* Levi S. Andrews, *now nearly thirty days overdue from Norfolk to Savannah. From the time the* Andrews *left Norfolk, now some twenty-eight days ago, no report of her has been received at the Virginia city, at Savannah or at the office of commissioner of navigation in Washington.*

Lillian had been frantic to hear from Abram. She didn't know that he had left Norfolk, and she called everyone she knew who might have heard from him. Finally, in late March, she received a call from Abram's brother, Frederick, who told her that Abram's ship had been given up for lost. She had feared it was so. She was heartbroken. No one could console her.

On July 16, 1914, the District Court of Pennsylvania issued the following decree:

> *A collision occurred at sea at night, on February 3 1913, between the schooner* City of Georgetown *and the steamship* Prinz Oskar, *in which the former was sunk. The evidence showed that her lights were burning and she kept her course and speed. The night was clear, and seeing that the steamer continued to approach some minutes before the collision, the mate took a torch and cast a light on the schooner's sails to attract attention. The steamer kept her speed of 12 knots until collision, and changed her course only when it was too late to avoid it. Her only lookout was stationed in the crow's nest, 98 feet from the stem and 81 feet above the water. The lookout saw the light cast on the schooner's sails, and twice reported the same, but the officers, who were busy laying the steamer's course for the voyage, paid no attention to it. When they finally saw the schooner's lights, no change of course was made for half a minute.*
>
> *HELD, that the schooner was not at fault; that the steamer was in fault for failure to keep out of the way, as required by Article 20 of the International Rules; for failure to have a lookout properly stationed; for failure of the officers to observe a proper degree of attention; and for failure to promptly reverse when the schooner was seen.*

Lillian and her daughter seated on a mast of the *City of Georgetown. Courtesy of Maine Maritime Museum.*

The owners of the *Prinz Oskar* appealed the decision of the District Court, but on January 8, 1915, the Circuit Court of Appeals upheld the lower court's decision without exception.

Lillian and Marjorie continued to live in Somerville, Massachusetts. On a wall of Lillian's bedroom hung the photograph that Abram had taken of her and Marjorie in 1902, seated on what would become the masts of his schooner *City of Georgetown.* Beside it was a poem that Abram had treasured:

I Must Go Down to the Sea

I must go down to the seas again, to the lonely sea and the sky,
   And all I ask is a tall ship and a star to steer her by,
And the wheel's kick and the wind's song and the white sail's shaking,
   And a grey mist on the sea's face and a grey dawn breaking.

I must go down to the seas again, for the call of the running tide
Is a wild call and a clear call that may not be denied;
And all I ask is a windy day with the white clouds flying,
And the flung spray and the blown spume, and the sea-gulls crying.

I must go down to the seas again, to the vagrant gypsy life,
To the gull's way and the whale's way where the wind's like a
whetted knife;
And all I ask is a merry yarn from a laughing fellow-rover,
And a quiet sleep and a sweet dream when the long trick's over.

John Masefield
1902

About the Author

The author and his three sons paint the bottom of their 1962 wooden cutter *Exodus* on Father's Day 2012. *Courtesy of Mary McAlister.*

Mac McAlister and his wife, Mary, live at Belle Isle Plantation in Georgetown, South Carolina. They cruised on sailboats for thirty years and now participate in the activities of the South Carolina Maritime Museum. Mac previously wrote *Cruising Through Life* and *Wooden Ships on Winyah Bay*.

Visit us at
www.historypress.net